TICKET TO THE GALLOWS

○ SILVER LINK RAILWAY ANTHOLOGIES ○

TICKET TO THE GALLOWS

and other villainous tales from the tracks

○ Barry Herbert ○

• CHILLERS, THRILLERS AND ECCENTRICS •
from
The NOSTALGIA *Collection*

To my Mother
whose support was so vital

A Silver Link book
from
The NOSTALGIA *Collection*

First published as *All Staions to Murder* in 1994
This edition first published 2001

British Library Cataloguing in Publication Data

ISBN 1 85794 088 1

Silver Link Publishing Ltd
The Trundle
Ringstead Road
Great Addington
Kettering
Northants NN14 4BW

Tel/Fax: 01536 330588
email: sales@nostalgiacollection.com
Website: www.nostalgiacollection.com

Printed and bound in Great Britain

Contents

Acknowledgements   7
Introduction   9

Part One: Small Beginnings
1   No smoking   13
2   Wartime fiddles   16
3   The opportunist   20
4   Revenge   23
5   The fire-raiser   26
6   A rum tale   28

Part Two: Robbery
7   Two in one night   29
8   The lure of gold   32
9   The Irish Mail train robbery   37
10   The good life and the clerk   41
11   The ticket fraud   44
12   Parcel pilferage   46
13   Operation Antler   49
14   The affair at Calton Loop   52
15   The joy-riders   55

Part Three: Grievous Bodily Harm
16   Railway riots and the navvies   59
17   Violence at Mark Beech   67
18   The fatal error   71
19   'This man has to be caught'   76
20   The bridge   80
21   The bombers   82

Part Four: Murder
22   'In the execution of his duty'   85
23   The murder of Railway Detective Hibbs   89

24	The ladder gang	92
25	Justice shall be seen to be done!	96
26	'This rotten crime'	102
27	Ticket to the gallows	106
28	Death in the goods yard	109
29	The last resort	112
30	The body in the tunnel	115
31	Death in carriage No 69	118
32	'It's been a lovely day!'	122
33	'I want money!'	127
34	Mrs East's last journey	130
35	The sad case of Arthur Mead	134
36	Mademoiselle est mort	138
37	The lost hours	141
38	Murder on the 9.02	144
39	The riddle of the black trunk	149
40	The tale of two trunks	154
41	The murderous scoundrel	158
42	Caught by telegraph	163
43	The Ballybrophy murder	167
44	Murder on the Limerick goods	170
45	Little boy lost, little boy murdered	177
46	The St Albans tragedy	180
47	Two peas in a pod	184
48	Deadly infatuation	187
49	Culpable homicide on the Aberdeen express	190

Acknowledgements

*M*y grateful thanks to Fred Guilliatt, Ian Forder, all at *Rail News*, particularly Paul Whiting, the Wrottesley family for encouragement and support, Bob Pacey and Steve Broughton at Lincoln, British Rail, which in all its facets gave me leads to obtain material, and my good friend Chris Bates, without whom no book can be written!

Thanks also to Brian Anderson, Alan Whitaker, Craig Cochrane, who tried to help me in Leeds, Janet Nicholson and Clive Darke, who gave assistance in getting the manuscript into shape, Mike Esau, for his encouragement, Dick Evans, Mike Furness, Brian Willey, and the BTP Archive at Tadworth.

I am grateful for permission to use summarised material from *The Vauxhall Murder* by Canon J. A. R. Brookes, fragments of material attributed to R. Whittington-Egan, *Co-incidence of Corpses* by Jonathan Goodman, *Death of a Countess* by Ivan Butler, *The Trial of John Alexander Dickman* by S. O. Rowan-Hamilton, and *The Merstham Tunnel Case* by Hargrave Lee Adam.

I am also grateful to other kind people who from time to time have assisted me with answers to many questions.

A very special thanks to Inspector Michael Morris for his tremendous help when all seemed so hopeless.

If I have missed anyone, please accept my apologies and thanks all the same.

I dedicate this book to my good friend John Wrottesley and my Mother, without whose encouragement and help all sorts of problems might have occurred to prevent me completing the book.

Introduction

*W*hen I was a boy – it seems a long time ago! – in Harrogate, there was a main railway line in the area. My friends and I were trainspotters; we were also criminals, as we were fascinated by the effect of a steam locomotive's driving wheels on a penny or halfpenny. We would creep through the wire fence, place the coin on the line, then retire to a good vantage point and watch as the 'B1', 'Hunt' or 'Shire' Class loco on a seven-coach passenger train would approach and flatten the coin into a very incongruous shape. Funnily enough, we never saw a freight train to flatten our coins – I wonder why.

Anyway, we were committing a criminal act although we probably did not realise the danger we faced by trespassing on a very busy main line. Today we hear of many examples of criminal vandalism, such as obstacles being placed across the tracks by people who have no thought of the damage and danger that such an act could result in, and young children whose delight after school is running to the nearby railway bridge and pelting bricks at the locos as they pass beneath. Several drivers have been badly hurt by such objects; perhaps the children do not realise what they are doing – life is a game and the danger does not register.

Recently an act of highly dangerous vandalism happened when two heavy steel flanges were suspended just beneath a bridge. One of the new 'Electra' Class electric locomotives hit these obstacles at speed; they tore through the roof and just missed the driver's head. Other recent reports of children and youths putting sleepers across the line, or hurling large pebbles at passing trains, mainly diesel multiple units, breaking windows.

The act of trespass has never been sorted out to the public's satisfaction. The main reason for the denial of access to railway property is predominantly for the public's own protection, especially in these days of high-voltage cables and other equipment that has to be kept isolated from the public. Anywhere near a railway line there lurks danger, be it from a slowly moving wagon or a silent-running electric locomotive – the public must respect the potential danger. Even stations are potential danger areas when a train pulls in or departs – not all passengers are so careful, and some try to jump on or get off the train while it is in motion. Likewise, many people disregard the warnings and stick their heads out of the window while the train is speeding along, and many have lost that appendage as a result of their folly.

Theft of railway property is as old as the railways themselves. Isolated railway sidings are still susceptible to break-ins and the theft of virtually any item the thief fancies. Years ago, light bulbs and the pretty water colours would be stolen from the old compartment stock – they were fair game and nearly everybody knew someone who had one! Today the emphasis is on much more valuable items – parcels are a major target, and the thieves seem to know just where to strike. Parcels have been a popular target since the inception of railways, and the most stringent methods to deter thieves have been employed by both British Rail and the Post Office, but still they are lost. It must be very difficult to stop this constant theft.

The light-fingered brigade now plan their nefarious activities very thoroughly, hence the success of the so-called Great Train Robbery in the 1960s. It is clear that this bold crime must have been planned down to the last detail, and while such blatant crime thrills the public at the time, it cannot fail to cast doubt upon the system that allows it to happen. We in this country are very good at closing the stable door after the horse has bolted; in so many cases of crime, security has been tightened up *after* the crime has occurred.

In the old steam days the sheds were very vulnerable and were visited on many occasions by thieves who would help themselves to many items such as copper, lead, brass, etc, found lying around. Such visitors were hard to keep out as they usually had a 'friend' on the inside to tip them off as to what might be found. It was also known for children to find ways of entering Motive Power Depots and actually clambering up on to the footplate of steam locomotives and moving them; the same escapade has been seen to happen on modern-day diesels, and the potential danger of these serious incidents hardly bears thinking about! Today burglaries of stores in Railway Depots are as frequent as ever, the main target still seeming to be copper and brass, and stories are told in the London area of wagons in sidings being robbed of their phosphor-bronze bearings.

No less criminal was the act of stealing fittings and other items from the scores of redundant steam locomotives stored in countless remote sidings during the indecent haste to replace steam with diesel traction in the late 1960s. Any trivial failure seemed to be enough to condemn a loco to the scrapyard to be cut up, and during this time the collectors would descend on these engines in droves and remove plates and fittings. The authorities soon became aware of the wholesale thieving that went on and security was stepped up, gates were locked, and the Railway Police showed more of a presence, but still the stealing went on. It would seem that everyone wanted a relic of the steam age, and even subsequently the diesel age, and trade in such objects today provides a lucrative market – but one does sometimes wonder if the items offered for sale have been obtained by legal means.

Fare-dodging continues to cause many problems, and hiding in the toilet does not seem to work these days as the Railway Police are wise to such dodges. Another kind of criminal from days gone by was the card sharp, who made such a good living swindling innocent punters on the express trains in the 1920s and '30s. Gambling for money on a train would seem to be an illegal act, but it was practised by the expert card manipulators who could spot a wealthy dupe a mile away. The sharps would usually work in pairs and would persuade the innocent to join them in a game of 'chance'. The method was that the victim won a few times, then was persuaded by the sharp to put a bigger stake on 'finding the lady', and this was his undoing because the sharp always won. On one occasion a pair of sharps made a major error in asking a certain mug to chance his luck on a crowded Scottish express one dark winter's night. The crooks let the victim win quite a lot, then suggested that the stakes should be trebled to 'have a real game'. Not only did the passenger win, but he turned out to be a Railway Police Officer who had been deputed to find the swindlers and curtail their activities.

There are not many Railway Policemen to cover the whole of the British Isles, yet they seem to cope very well under the circumstances, dovetailing successfully with civil police forces, and although there seem to be more cases of reported crime on Britain's railways, there are also more cases that have been dealt with in a satisfactory manner. The very magnitude of cases of railway crime never ceases to amaze, but as technology improves the system for catching the criminal, he can also use the same technology to commit the crime.

The strength of the British Transport Police force is 2,041 men, and they have to police the whole of the railway network of 11,500 miles. Considering how thinly spread this force is, it is amazing how they cope; the fact that they are so highly organised helps them to become involved throughout the system. The following figures give some indication of the magnitude of the task facing them: in 1991 there were four passenger murders, three attempted murders, three stabbings, 129 cases of grievous bodily harm, 137 cases of malicious wounding, 1,630 cases of actual bodily harm, 14 cases of rape, 427 cases of indecent assault, 1,401 cases of robbery from passengers, 8,412 cases of actual theft from persons connected with travelling on the system, and 224 cases of theft of mail in transit.

Both passengers and staff are potential victims of the less law-abiding elements of our society, from a case of annoying drunkenness to far more serious attacks. Think just how vulnerable the lone conductor/guard and his handful of passengers are on a two-car DMU in the depths of the country, especially after dark. . .

The research for this book has resulted in near complete hair loss! Information was so hard to find until one day the doors opened and the flood commenced. Here you will find a rare mixture of items and incidents of railway-related crime of all kinds. The solutions of the many incidents have also been many and varied; modern forensic methods do help the law to perform its duties better, and more conclusive results are more satisfactory and acceptable.

This book deals predominantly with murder in all its forms. However, many other kinds of crime such as robbery, trespass and even taking away items of rolling-stock are included.

It is also fascinating to read the accounts of some of the murder trials, absorb the evidence and possibly arrive at other conclusions. If one takes into account that someone's life or death often hinged on the evidence, readers will find themselves both judge and jury.

This record of crime on the railways has been my 'magnum opus' and the product of two years' work, so I hope readers will share my fascination in this subject.

Part One: Small Beginnings

1
No smoking

*L*et us start with a relatively minor offence (depending on whether you're a smoker or not!). Such is the craving experienced by the majority of smokers in their addiction to the foul weed that travellers by rail will do almost anything to ensure that they can indulge their smoking in peace as they travel, and in the middle and late 1800s the smokers' wiles were most ingenious, as we shall see.

As far back as 1868 a clause was introduced into the Railway Regulations Bill making it imperative on the part of the various railway companies to put a smoking carriage in every train that consisted of more than one carriage of each class. Consequently, to appease the non-smokers every company with any thought as to the promotion of its train service adopted the by-law that any person smoking in covered accommodation or areas that have been regarded as exempt from the enjoyment of the weed should be liable to a penalty not exceeding 40 shillings.

No doubt the foreign visitor travelling by train between London and Brighton in 1842 enjoying his expensive cigar was most upset when the Guard approached warning him that he was breaking the law. He waved the Guard away and continued to puff on his cigar, but at the next station he was ordered out of the train and was asked for his ticket. Then came the terrible statement addressed to a porter by the Guard: 'This person shall not be permitted to travel to Brighton by any train this night'. So the foreign visitor was left stranded at a minor station for the night for refusing to obey the Regulations laid down for all to observe governing the smoking of strong tobacco.

Then there is the tale of the Eton pupils crowding into a compartment and smoking cigarettes with no regard for the quiet old man who was sitting in a corner, asking them to refrain from 'the devil's weed'. They took no notice whatsoever and laughed at his entreaties, so the old man pulled out a short black pipe and proceeded to stuff it with thick black twist. His eyes twinkled as he lit up, making sure that the windows were tightly shut. The boys watched him with anticipation, then the clouds of acrid, foul-smelling smoke billowed up and filled the compartment with the odour of 'Old Tom'. The old gentlemen made sure that the boys filled their lungs with the fumes and watched them go green around the gills as the strong tobacco got at them. The Etonians then became strangely quiet; they could not get out of the compartment, trapped by the old man who would see that they did not forget their experience.

The strait-laced old lady sitting primly in the 1st Class compartment reading her book was horrified when a roughly dressed man burst in as the train pulled out of the station. He sat down opposite her, looked her up and down, leered at her with broken, yellow teeth, then brought out a large pipe and started to fill it with black twist. He put the unlit pipe in his pocket and leered at the lady again; she did not return his smile but looked very grim and her looks showed her disapproval at his very presence.

'I don't suppose you'll mind if I light me pipe, luv?'

She bridled up. 'Indeed I do, and you've no business to come into this compartment with *that* thing.' She pointed a quivering finger at his pipe.

The man laughed, a coarse, loud laugh. He fumbled in his pocket for a vesta, lit his pipe and blew evil-smelling smoke across the compartment, regarding her in her discomfort.

'I paid me fare, and all the other carriages are full up, so I'm here and if you don't like it you'd better git off at the next stop.'

A lady who travelled by train regularly from London to Macclesfield told of her experiences travelling on the railway in the 1870s. One particular day, the train, composed of four- and six-wheeled compartment stock, pulled into Longsight station near Manchester. The lady ran along the platform looking for a suitable seat, but she could only find a 2nd Class smoking compartment. It was not quite full so she decided to risk entering. It contained three gentlemen, one of whom was smoking.

The lady pursed her lips and said, 'Gentlemen, I do not willingly intrude, but I have never before seen such a long train with so many 2nd Class smoking compartments and only one 2nd Class non-smoking compartment.'

The three men smiled. The lady was puzzled, but soon understood the situation. A few stations later, after the train had passed Stockport, the man who was smoking folded his rug and newspaper and, among his other preparations for leaving the train, peeled the 'Smoking' sign from the window and carefully placed it inside the lining of his hat – for further use!

The lady was most anxious to know how he came about the notices for 'Smoking' and 'No Smoking', as this was an infringement of the railway's Rules and Regulations, so when she reached her home she looked in her brother's business hat and sure enough there were two 'Smoking' labels. When she asked him about the notices he gave her a wink and said, 'Friends at court – all my fellow travellers have them and find them very handy.'

Incidentally, the 'No Smoking' signs on the windows of passenger carriages gave the father of that fine actor and light comedian Jack Watson the idea for a change of name. A very famous Music Hall comedian, he travelled the British Isles under the name of Vernon Watson until one day he fancied he might boost his reputation with a change of name and image. He was travelling by train to another theatre and was day-dreaming while looking at the passing countryside. He did not smoke much, but on occasions a cigar was very pleasant, and he happened to study the sign on the carriage window and the thought came to him that 'Nosmo King' would be an original name for a Music Hall comedian, so from that day he was known by that stage name.

In these days of High Speed Trains, 'Sprinters' and 'Pacers' the smoker is frowned upon and very little space is provided in the modern carriage, while the contradictory arguments still prevail: Central Government wants the lucrative tax derived from selling tobacco to the public, while fierce charges emanating from the health authorities remind us that smoking kills.

2
Wartime fiddles

More 'petty crime', but some that was serious enough to railway employees at the time. September 1939 brought the call to arms to defend the realm against the armed forces of Hitler's Germany, who were sure that Britain would not want to be dragged into a long war. Hitler also thought, quite wrongly, that Great Britain would acquiesce to his march into Poland to reclaim land taken away from the Fatherland after the 1914-18 war.

That month also saw the staff of Britain's railway companies co-operating to move an unimaginable volume of both passenger and goods traffic to every part of the United Kingdom. Conflict did, however, break out between the railway authorities and the armed forces over the issue of travel warrants for going on leave; those on short passes (say 48 hours) were expected to pay their own fares. This produced an enormous volume of penniless conscripts trying to get to their homes as best they could, and the people concerned certainly used their initiative to outwit the railway authorities on many occasions. Road travel was very restricted and unreliable, as petrol was, of course, rationed and private cars were few and far between, while public services were over-used and the timings vague. The railway alone gave some reliability under the adverse conditions, and the staff that operated the system worked like heroes as the train took the strain.

Initiative, imagination and resolve are the qualities that are expected of those that wage war, and these attributes were brought to bear on every ticket collector in the land – the railway plotters were kept very busy 'doctoring' tickets that would convince the authorities, and these experts could, with the aid of some mysterious chemical, alter the date and destination of those little bits of green cardboard that spelled 'liberty'. Needless to say, these craftsmen required a substantial reward for their esteemed services, usually a vast amount of cigarettes or a rare bottle of, dare I say it, Scotch! Often the artist would agree a price for the job and could dictate his own terms – the customer would just pay up!

When it came to getting in and out of stations, men's ingenuity knew no bounds – holes in hedges, fences, underground, overground, there were usually ways of getting on to a station platform and then into a train without a ticket. There would be a network of information concerning all the main-line termini covering such things as alternative exits, climbable walls and so on; the servicemen soon knew how to avoid 'Old Crabface' on the ticket barrier, but 'Silly Billy' was a much more easy touch and was very easy to fool or confuse. How all this data was collected and fed along the grapevine nobody knew; it just became common knowledge because So-and-so said so.

It was a really complicated system. There was, for instance, a major loophole in the LMS schedule for the afternoon train from Euston to Birmingham New Street. Both of these were 'open' stations, which meant that they had no ticket barrier; tickets were checked on the train en route, Now, had this exercise been carried out when the train was in motion it would have been quite satisfactory, but for some strange reason the ticket collector passed through the coaching stock while the train was standing in Birmingham station, which meant that one could get off the train and have a sandwich and a cup of tea in the station buffet and then, after a leg-stretch, wander back to the train which was filling up with passengers. It is doubtful if there was a single 'Brummie' Serviceman who was not aware of this highly convenient arrangement.

Of course, tickets would also switch hands, and the ticket collector would be satisfied that the one-ticket-per-man rule was being observed. Little did he know that the same ticket had been presented to him several times by a bunch of sweaty servicemen who surrounded him pushing and shoving. The ticket collector was only too pleased to get off the 14-coach train; he did not like the job of passing among the boys in blue or khaki, as they knew too much of how to 'buck' the system.

But how does our friend the collector handle around 200 sailors, all milling around the ticket barrier on Parkestone Quay? This was the regular problem of the little old collector who used to be known as 'Grandad' to the matelots. He once tried to 'channel' them towards the gate by blocking the platform with trolleys, but they climbed over them and he was swept aside and lost in the wave of dark blue-uniformed bodies. He knew that many of them had no tickets, but how to stop them?

One night he enlisted the help of the Station Master and a porter, but as the dark blue tide drew closer, the railway staff turned and fled. This intimidating mob was in fact good-humoured and bore no ill will or animosity to 'Grandad', but regarded the whole affair as a legitimate sport, even though the odds were distinctly unfair. The main cause of the trouble usually arrived on the last train from Dovercourt. This train was unofficially dubbed the 'Drunks Express', but it could have been equally known as the 'Ghost Train', for it was little more than a skeleton, having been stripped of all moveable fittings – the windows had gone, seats ripped and loosened, light bulbs gone, they had gone berserk. Talk about football fans wrecking trains – this wartime lot could teach any present-day vandal a trick or two. Some of the passengers on this spartan train were very drunk, some silly with it, some very aggressive, but they all had to disembark from the wrecked carriages and hopefully produce a ticket to show 'Grandad', who was sober. Such were the problems of a ticket collector!

A much more civilised arrangement was made at Colchester. The town had no YMCA hostel, and the authorities had persuaded the LNER to allow the troops to bed down in the carriages of a certain stationary train. They were even supplied with a 'knocker- up' who would fling wide every door and yell 'Let's 'ave yer, then!'. Now and again some slumbering soldier or airman would be overlooked and he would wake to find himself halfway to London when he should have been back at his camp. It is worth noting that the men did very little damage to these coaches, known as 'The Sleeping Car Service'.

The art of evading the travelling ticket collector en route became refined in time. One would think that there was no escape, but the servicemen soon found ways and means of giving the poor soul who had the job of collecting the tickets a hard time! One way, operating a sort of 'tic-tac' warning system, became a thoroughly polished art, and would be employed to issue a warning when the 'Ogre' was on his way. The usual methods of concealing the ticket-less were a) on the luggage rack behind some kitbags, b) under the seat where you risked a nasty burn from the heater, or c) huddled in the farthest corner of the seats by your mates and invisible to the 'Ogre'; this latter dodge called for a small person.

Some dare-devils went out and clung to the side of the carriage, which was extremely dangerous. 'Drop-off' was also fraught with danger – this was when one jumped from a moving train as it slowed down to enter a station. It called for a lot of courage as well as an intimate knowledge of speeds, gradients and, above all, the location of soft landings. It has been known for chaps to 'drop off' close to their homes, thus saving time as well as a ticket; it was a moot point whether an injury sustained in this way could be classified as a war wound. . . Last but not least is the noble art of toilet cramming – six men in a toilet was not unknown, but the record is thought to have been ten!

Sometimes the military ticket presented to the long-suffering collector was genuine, having been bought with a whip-round among the gang, If, on the other hand, they were able to use a 'doctored' ticket, the whole operation could be judged a total success in the prosecution of swindling the railway companies, although not exactly helping them in the very good job they were doing in keeping communications running.

3
The opportunist

A derailment, however minor, on any part of the railway system usually causes some inconvenience and disruption of services to the frustration of passengers whose journey is inevitably interrupted. Such a derailment occurred near Flax Burton, south-west of Bristol, when some loaded coal wagons left the track, causing both up and down lines to be blocked between Bristol and Weston-Super-Mare. The coal was spread over a wide area of the surrounding land, and the incident resulted in BR having to run an emergency bus service between the two places, which would be required to call at all stations en route.

On the day of the derailment the owner of the bus company that had been given the contract was visited by a very impressive young man, smartly dressed and with an air of astute and sensible responsibility, who told the owner that he was from British Rail and that he had been authorised by the Area Manager to set in motion the emergency bus service. The young man gave the owner instructions as to how to proceed with the arrangements, and left.

The man from the bus company was very impressed with his visitor's knowledge of the situation, and was confident that all seemed correct and under control. The service ran fluently, the buses called at the railway stations along the route, and the young man was often seen organising the transfer from bus to train. He seemed popular with the passengers, and even turned out late at night at the various stations during the three-day emergency. Everyone seemed very taken by his charm and pleasant approach. However, it seemed somewhat strange that during the emergency, and in spite of his presence at the hub of the operation, nobody questioned his authority or credibility regarding his position within British Rail. Indeed, most people agreed that he had done a good job in organising the smooth running of the bus service and the transfer of passengers between the two towns, and the travelling public were, for once, impressed by BR's organisation.

For example, on one occasion, at Yatton station, passengers were awaiting the arrival of the bus to travel to Bristol, but it had been delayed and the travellers were getting impatient. Our friend arrived and was told of the delay, and that the coach drivers were taking their break. He found them in a pub, ordered them back into the coaches, had them pick up the frustrated passengers and got them on their way. On the second day after the derailment the efficient young man showed his generosity when he saw eight factory workers waiting for their train to Newport; the derailment had not affected the train services to South Wales from Bristol, but our young man seemed upset that these workers were having to wait for half an hour for their train, so he decided to help them. He telephoned the bus company and ordered a 53-seater luxury coach to take the men to Severn Tunnel Junction. The men were very grateful for this show of concern and the rapid remedy.

After this act of understanding and public spiritedness the young man thought he would go to the scene of the derailment and see how the job was going on to clear the mess and repair the damaged line. He arrived in some comfort in a chauffeur-driven car, and on arrival talked to the supervisors and technical men and represented himself as the Area Manager! What is more, the railway personnel accepted the fact that this was indeed who he was.

He now decided that it was time that he should receive some reward for his hard work in keeping things moving smoothly, so he decided to sell some of the coal that was scattered around the scene of the derailment. There were plenty of takers among the railway staff; he charged them 25p per hundredweight and assured the purchasers that all the money would be donated to a charity. There were so many demands for the coal at the 'knock-down' price that he was taking a lot of money; he also arranged for one of the wagons that had left the track to be sold to a scrap dealer. He even gave out receipts for the sale of the coal; as it was to turn out, it was a good job that no railway police officers were offered the coal, which would have been very embarrassing!

The young man's professional cover was becoming ever thinner, and the owner of the bus company had been rather suspicious when the booking of the luxury coach for the eight workers was made. He therefore thought that he should check for verification of this booking. The real Area Manager was told, and it was found that the bogus one had no authority whatsoever. The bluff had been discovered.

So who was this young man who had performed so efficiently? Enquiries were made and the railway police were called in. Suspicions soon centred on a 29-year-old fanatical trainspotter, who was traced and arrested at his home. When he was interviewed about the whole affair, he admitted being involved and he was charged with a number of offences under Sections 15 and 16 of the Theft Act 1968. About 5 minutes before he was due to appear before Bristol Magistrates it became known that he was alleged to have been responsible for other offences in the Cardiff area, but as he was not wanted on warrant the Magistrates at Bristol fined him a total of £80 for the offences he committed on the railway, then the railway police re-arrested him to take him to Cardiff.

His past record of illegal activities became known, and it appeared that he had spoken to a number of young boys who were trainspotting at Cardiff General station and told them that he was organising a coach trip to go spotting in Scotland; a few of the boys actually sent money to the man's home for this trip. The coach, of course, did not appear to pick them up as promised. Further information revealed that the accused had also approached a number of passengers at Derby station and informed them that he was arranging a trip for trainspotters; again money was sent to him at his home. All these offences were known to the railway police.

So here was an enterprising young man who, because of his charm and easy manner, seemed to convince the public of his decency and reliability; certainly he could take people in and was, as we have seen, able to impress others with his organisational ability. Perhaps one could say that his enthusiasm just ran away with him!

4
Revenge

*T*he previous story demonstrated that there are some people for whom the operation of our railway system provides continual interest, although amongst them are those who cannot stop themselves from trying to find out how everything works; this usually means trespassing on railway property to examine equipment at closer quarters, which is a very dangerous practice not to be recommended. But the most lethal are those members of the public who take a delight in putting things on the track or jamming points with bits of wood to see what will happen. This exciting pastime often has terrible consequences, and is exactly what the railway is continually on its guard against.

To illustrate this we will tell the story of a man who joined British Railways as a trainee conductor some years ago. Not content with his job of learning the finer points of his particular job, he found some fascination in walking along the track, and was frequently stopped and asked his business. He would reply that he was on his way to or from work. The railway police were, however, suspicious, and decided to keep an eye on his movements, especially near the railway. His odd behaviour also persuaded his supervisors that he was not the right man for the job, and after considerable thought and consultation they decided that he was unsuitable for employment on BR.

This rebuff to his ambitions seems to have triggered a desire for some sort of revenge in the man's mind; he obviously thought that he was dismissed unfairly and that he was not given enough time to settle into the job. He may have been right, but it would appear that he had not shown the correct aptitude and there were plenty of other candidates who were in line for the position.

Whatever, his dismissal obviously preyed on his mind and he seemed determined to find some way to wreak revenge on the railway. Then things started to happen. One Saturday a track circuit failure registered on the panel in a signal box, and investigations revealed that an electric track circuit cable had been placed across the track in various places and had been severed by passing trains, with the result that services were disrupted. District CID officers now became involved to investigate the cause of the incident, but they drew a blank.

Two days later once again a failure was recorded on the panel at the signal box, and again investigations were carried out. Many people were interviewed, and it was again found that a track circuit cable had been placed over the rails and the next train in the section had cut it; trains were delayed and the timetable disrupted.

The local police joined forces with the CID to try to find the perpetrator of these crimes. This time, as the result of the joint effort, some success was achieved. Enquiries were made at the local rail depot to ask drivers if they had seen anyone either walking on or near the tracks in daylight hours; it then became known that our friend the ex-trainee had been seen on the embankment on two occasions just before dark, and this news was passed on to the railway police. It was learned soon afterwards that he had been arrested on a charge of arson the previous night; the charge involved the setting on fire of a wooden building in the local cemetery that lay adjacent to the exact place of the last severed track circuit cable.

The railway police interviewed the man for 4 hours concerning his possible involvement, but he denied everything – he avowed that he had not been near the track, and he had not touched the cable. But then he cracked and admitted that he had pulled the cable apart, but claimed that it was an accident, and he had merely wanted to make sure that the cable was safe. He was nonetheless cautioned and charged with the two offences of obstructing the railway contrary to the Malicious Damage Act 1861 Section 36, and two offences under the Criminal Damage Act 1971.

He subsequently appeared at the local Magistrates Court, and although he pleaded not guilty he was committed for trial, but allowed bail. Ten days later another track failure was recorded in the panel box, and the fault was traced once more to a severed track circuit cable that had been laid across the track at a nearby bridge; again train services were disrupted and inconvenience caused to the travelling public. The man was seen by the police, but his wife and daughter insisted that at the time of the occurrence he was at home. The police, however, were not satisfied and decided to keep the house under surveillance. Of course, during this period of observation the man did not go near the railway, and after a few days the watch was called off.

At 11 pm one Sunday a couple of weeks later there was an incident that showed that all was not over by far. A passenger train travelling at high speed hit a large concrete block that had been placed across the track near a bridge. Fortunately there were no injuries, although the passengers were badly shaken. The man was interviewed again and denied any knowledge of the incident, challenging the police to come up with some proof. Again a watch was kept on his house at night. The police realised that they were dealing with an unstable and potentially dangerous man who would stop at nothing, and who, if he was not restrained, could cause a very serious accident.

In due course the man appeared in court and entered a plea of guilty to the arson charge but not guilty to the charges brought against him by the British Transport Police. The Recorder ordered the charge of not guilty to remain on the Court file, but the man was placed on probation for the arson charge. Subsequently no other obstructions or similar incidents occurred in the area, although following the trial it is said that he admitted to the other charges in an attempt to get revenge for being dismissed from his job.

5
The fire-raiser

One sunny late June day a few years ago a young man hopped aboard a local two-car diesel train. He was unemployed, a bit of a tearaway, couldn't keep a job and was easily bored; and boredom with some people can be dangerous. He soon turned to crime, mainly to obtain money to supplement his benefit, which was soon spent in the local pub where he had incurred the wrath of the tenant; barred from entering the building on many occasions, he had taken his revenge by smashing several windows and committing other damage to the premises. However, he found the other local in the village more to his liking, and had so far refrained from misbehaviour, although alcohol had become somewhat of a problem and his resultant drunken, erratic manners made him a person to avoid.

The train was virtually empty, the guard was talking to the driver most of the journey, and our friend had most of the coach to himself. Becoming bored, he looked around for something to do. He wandered through the brake compartment, where he saw the guard's jacket hanging, moving to and fro with the motion of the train. He couldn't believe his luck, and he rifled through the pockets. The most interesting thing he found was a bunch of keys, which he kept after throwing the other items from the jacket out of the window. The guard was still in deep conversation with the driver.

On reaching his destination the lad was seen to leave the station, his unkempt appearance registered by the ticket collector. He went into the nearest pub and examined the keys – a small tag attached to one of them told him that they were for the buildings at the station. After a few pints he left the pub and walked around the town looking in shop windows. He later found a seat and dropped off to sleep, later visiting another pub where he found a few of his pals. One drink led to another, and soon he became very drunk and very unpleasant He staggered out of the pub and returned to the station.

That night the local fire brigade was called to a fire at the station at 11.30 pm. The person making the 999 call gave his name as Mr Fielding, with a local address, but this proved to be false; he also gave a false phone number. The fire had been started in a mess room, and the damage was severe, gutting the room and causing damage to the tune of several thousand pounds. Another fire had been started in the diesel store, known as the pump room, but fortunately only slight damage was caused.

A search of the station was made and the intoxicated lad was found pretending to be asleep in a diesel train at the back of the premises. When challenged by the police he said, 'I've been done for arson twice before'.

He was arrested and taken to the Police Station where he was put in a cell. He was searched and the police found the bunch of keys. When interviewed he admitted stealing the bunch of keys from the guard's pocket, and said it was possible that he had started the fires but he couldn't remember.

He was again interviewed the next day about the alarm call, and admitted that he was the person who had rung the fire brigade. At his trial, when it was indicated that he would plead guilty to the theft of the keys but not guilty to the two counts of arson, the jury failed to agree on a verdict and were discharged. An application was made for the accused to be detained under Section 5 of the Mental Health Act 1983, and at the re-trial it was agreed that the two counts of arson be left on file. The alleged fire-raiser spent some time receiving treatment, but on his release he was once again suspected of committing arson on British Rail property.

6
A rum tale

*F*inally in this section, here is an amusing little story of how to obtain a drop of rum from an old cask. It is not strictly legal, but very warming on a cold day. This particular story happened in an East Coast town. A large brewery used to ship in casks of rum by rail, and the empty casks would then be stored in a yard near the brewery. On occasions a cask would disappear; however, this rare event began to occur more regularly, but the reason was given that the casks rotted away and were burned. The railwaymen, however, had other purposes for the empty rum casks – it was found that the rum had soaked so far into the wood of the cask that when boiling water was poured in, the wood gave out quite a lot of the liquor; drinking a cup of tea or coffee with a little of the liquid from the cask gave it quite a kick.

So the plan emerged of obtaining one of the casks from the brewery yard and bringing it to one of the sleeper-built cabins used for the accommodation of railwaymen. This commodious building had a large fire grate at one end, a large table in the middle and around the sides lockers for the use of the staff; at one end a plank of wood rested on two old casks, draped with greatcoats to make it more comfortable. Sometimes the railway police would call in to have a cup of tea and a chat, and on one occasion they were investigating the theft of some of the rum casks from the brewery.

Most of the warming liquid, whether tea or coffee, had been laced with the rum drawn from the old casks, and while the police were telling the men in the cabin about their search for the casks they were sitting on the plank warming themselves with the watered-down rum. I wonder if they enjoyed their drink? Or is ignorance bliss?

Part Two: Robbery

7
Two in one night

This story concerns two robberies that exposed the trustful nature of the Great Western Railway Company, and also led to tighter vigilance of the conveyance of Her Majesty's Mail. In 1849 the conveyance of Royal Mail was considered the highest accolade of respectability and trust for any railway company, and the Great Western Railway was no exception, running its Mail Services with much efficiency and expedition. The very idea that a crook might find a way through the company's security system was unthinkable, but that year it happened, and the sheer simplicity with which the crooks were able to steal the contents of the Post Office Tender was incredible.

The Mail train between Plymouth and Paddington left Plymouth at 6.35 pm for the usual run to the capital. It consisted of six 1st and 2nd Class carriages, a Post Office sorting van and a Post Office Tender, where the full bags of mail were to be locked up. A regular service, the Mail train was an everyday event and played its part in the expanding Post Office function of delivering post and parcels throughout the British Isles.

At around 6.45 pm a coach approached the little station at Laira, where it stopped and two young men alighted, both well dressed and bewhiskered as was the vogue of the day. They booked 1st Class tickets to Bristol, then stood around in the shadows of the gas-lit station awaiting the arrival of their train. One of the men, Harry Poole, was anxious not to be noticed – he had been in the employ of the Great Western Railway but had been sacked for alleged theft. Nothing had been proved, but the circumstances seemed very strange and Poole had been unable to explain them to the satisfaction of the company, so he had been dismissed with a large question mark against his character. He did not want any of the station staff or footplate men to see him – they might put two and two together, and that would never do!

At last the train from Plymouth rolled in, the two men found an empty compartment next to the Post Office Tender and climbed in; simultaneously the Post Office sorting van was coupled up next to them. They watched as bulging bags of mail were loaded into the tender, then it was locked up. Poole and his friend, Edward Nightingale, the son of a well-known London bookmaker, settled themselves into the cushions and discussed the plans to effect their audacious robbery.

The train reached Exeter at 9 pm, on time; various people joined the train but no one seemed interested in getting into Poole and Nightingale's compartment, so they could relax. About an hour and a half later the train drew into Bridgwater and the two men stretched out their legs on the seats, feigning sleep, and again they were lucky as nobody got in. Out of the corner of his eye Nightingale watched more mail being loaded into the Post Office Tender. The train then moved off once more on its 40-mile journey to Bristol.

As it sped through the open countryside the two men swung into action. They opened the carriage door and, feeling their way along the narrow running-board to the Post Office Tender, Poole wrenched open the lock with a jemmy, and they climbed in. There they found the bags of mail and other valuables stowed in registered packages, and they quickly but calmly broke the seals and slit open the bags. Pulling out the registered packets and other potentially valuable items, they shoved their haul into two sacks that they had brought for the purpose. They worked fast and left a litter of ripped paper and open bags. The sounds of the robbery were drowned by the sound of the moving train, and the Post Office staff in the sorting van coupled to the tender were totally unaware of the audacious crime that was taking place in the next carriage.

Poole and Nightingale were keeping an eye on the time, and as the train had now began to slow down as it approached Bristol, they climbed down on to the running-boards and dropped off the train into soft grass with their sacks of loot. Imagine the surprise when the Guard opened the tender door to find the debris of the robbery; he looked in vain for the list of the registered packages and letters, but the two young men had taken that too! The station staff removed the remains of the mail, and what was left was taken to London later that night.

The perpetrators of the robbery hid their two sacks of loot at a safe location in Bristol and were now planning a *second* robbery that night. Just after 1 am we find them standing in the shadows of Bristol station, waiting for the ticket office to open. They thought they were alone, but unfortunately a very perceptive person was also waiting for a train. This was a Mr Lee, who lived at Clifton near Bristol, and he didn't miss a thing! He saw the men enter the station and saw them walk to an archway enveloped in deep shadows. Poole waited in the darkness as Nightingale walked over and tried the booking office door, but it was locked. The train was late and Lee made some comment to Nightingale to that effect, but the latter made no reply; either he had not heard or he just ignored the comment. Lee became more curious.

He kept his eye on the pair, who had meanwhile melted back into the shadows. At last the station bell rang to herald the approach of another Mail train, this time from Paddington. The booking office was opened, Lee followed the two young men through, and they bought their tickets. He then continued to follow them as they moved towards the end of the platform where the gas lights gave way to deep shadows; he could hear the sound of voices but could not see the speakers.

The train pulled in and the two thieves couldn't get aboard quickly enough! The guard had courteously opened a compartment door, but the two men had seen that someone else was in the compartment and had quickly found an empty one – near the Post Office Tender! Despite the fact that Lee found a seat where he could try to keep up his surveillance, the two men managed to repeat their previous robbery. And they might have got away with it, too, if it had not been for the observant Mr Lee, who, when the train reached Bridgwater, told the station staff of his suspicions about the two young men.

As a result, after a scuffle Poole and Nightingale were arrested and were found to be in possession of the stolen packets and valuables. The police remembered a gold bullion robbery that had astonished the nation earlier in that year; there were similarities between the two, so they suspected that Poole and Nightingale might have been also involved with that major crime.

Some 114 years later the trust that we place in Britain's railways as conveyors of the nation's mails was still being betrayed – in 1963 the so-called Great Train Robbery was only the latest in a series of audacious robberies that is as old as the railways themselves.

8
The lure of gold

Gold has always possessed a fatal attraction for all aspiring to riches – it represents the ultimate in precious metals, the most highly prized of possessions, and is the symbol for the highest standards of attainment. Small wonder then that the lure of obtaining gold by other than legal means has always occupied the minds of villains the world over.

As the emergent railways began to convey passengers and freight traffic all over the British Isles in the first half of the last century, it followed that at some time or other gold would be a commodity that would, under the strictest security, be assigned to rail transport. It also followed that the villains who sought to perpetrate crime on the railway system of the British Isles soon came up with ideas to relieve the railway companies of these precious consignments entrusted to their care. It therefore was not long before the first big gold robbery took place, which, incidentally, remains unsolved to this day.

The actual robbery happened between London and Bristol the year before the previous story, in 1848, and £1,500 worth of gold sovereigns were stolen. The stout wooden box, secured with iron bands and quite heavy, was delivered into the care of a guard at Paddington station by a messenger from a London bank. The guard put the box into a compartment that was next to his so that he could keep an eye on the precious cargo. In spite of these precautions, however, when the train arrived at Bristol the box was found to have been broken open and the coins had gone. just how this was done remains a complete mystery.

The Great Western Railway and the general public were horrified and disturbed by this serious loss, but seven years later an even more spectacular crime was committed that involved the theft of bullion worth more than £14,000. This audacious robbery was referred to for many years after as 'The Great Gold Robbery'.

Edward Agarr was a well educated, intelligent man of slight but impressive build. He looked as if he could be accurately termed a solid member of the Establishment and a pillar of Society. In fact, he was exactly the opposite, and he used his considerable talents to outwit the law. He was a friend of the corrupt barrister and forger, James Townsend Saward, known to the police as 'Jim the Penman', who was primarily responsible for organised crime in the London area for close on 25 years.

In 1848 Agarr met an employee of the South Eastern Railway named William Pierce, who was a printer and supplied the tickets for the railway. The two men had much in common – they both liked easy money and the best that money could buy. They used to meet in various pubs and would discuss ways and means of making the 'quick buck', but one of their more ambitious ideas, which was an important topic of their conversation, was whether it was possible to steal the gold bullion that travelled by train between London and the Continent.

Agarr learned quite a lot of useful information from Pierce regarding the movement of the bullion, but since the unsolved robbery seven years earlier the security of transit had been tightened up, so in the present circumstances the pair decided to forget the idea. For the time being. . .

Edward Agarr later went to America. What exactly he was doing over there is not quite certain, but we can be sure that his agile mind was taking in ideas that could be put to other than legal use. When he arrived back in England he sought out Pierce and they had several intense conversations, and we can guess that crime was the main topic on the agenda. The idea was a bullion robbery on a never-before-seen scale involving £14,000 worth of gold bullion.

Taking into consideration the now formidable security precautions employed by the railway companies throughout the country, any plans to break through these safeguards would have to be planned with almost military precision. Duplicate keys would be necessary for the travelling safes, and contact would have to be made with people who could be reliable and who had knowledge of the details of train movements, times, and the routine of railway staff. By this time Pierce had been sacked by the South Eastern Railway, and he was very keen to throw in his lot with Agarr and his criminal pals.

The methods of trans-shipping gold bullion from London to Folkestone, thence to the Continent, were complex, yet so far effective. The gold was loaded on to the night train from London. It was brought from the London goldsmiths in wooden boxes bound with metal, was weighed and sealed, then taken to London Bridge station. Once there, the boxes were transferred to travelling safes made of iron, each of which would have two patent locks; these safes were provided by the South Eastern Railway for the conveyance of valuables.

Agarr soon realised that he would have to find the weakest link in this security system chain that afforded maximum protection for valuables sent by the South Eastern Railway. Most of the staff working for the railway were honest, reliable and totally trustworthy men; they took a pride in their jobs and would do anything to promote the company's name and reputation. However, with Pierce's assistance Agarr tried to find a suitable ally in the company, someone who would show them the details of the gold shipments and whose loyalty could be relied upon. They found a railway guard called James Burgess.

The police was meanwhile keeping an eye on Mr Agarr. Inspector Hazell observed the comings and goings of Agarr and his friends, and warned his colleagues to look out for him, believing him to be a pickpocket. Agarr had seen the signs of police activity and decided to get lost in London for a while. He, Pierce and Burgess often met in pubs such as The Green Man and the White Hart in the City of London, then a stroke of luck came their way. Another of their accomplices, Mr Tester, the suave, dapper Station Master at Margate, was promoted to the same position at London Bridge. It could not have suited the villains better, for Tester was now in charge of the office that dealt with the shipment of valuable goods – very good news!

Strangely enough, Mr Tester found that one of the keys for the travelling safes needed replacement, and he saw to this personally and was able to give Agarr the key for him to obtain a wax impression. Now a copy of a second key was needed, and Agarr showed his nimble mind by sending a box containing bullion worth over £200 to a 'C. E. Archer', who of course was Edward Agarr. Agarr went back to Folkestone soon afterwards and took note of the activities in the office as the boat trains came in. He also made several trips over the Channel to see how traffic was processed on the Boulogne side, and travelled several times on the Night Mail when Burgess was on duty as the guard. This gave him the opportunity to test his duplicate keys in the safes.

The villains were now waiting for Tester to give them the word when a consignment of bullion was expected, and at last word came from the flamboyant little Station Master. Gold bullion was to be shipped from London to Paris on the night of 15 May 1855. Everything was ready. Agarr had bought 2 cwt of lead shot a few weeks before and it was packed into small bags and then into leather bags and the carpet bags that were the vogue of the time; in one of the carpet bags Agarr also placed a mallet, chisels, sealing wax and tapers.

Pierce was disguised with a wig and beard in case he should run into someone who knew him, and he and Agarr bought 1st Class tickets for the gold train; they even handed their heavy carpet bags to the porter to load on to the train. Agarr's luck was in – by sheer chance Burgess was guard on that train, and he let him into the guard's van as the train pulled out of London Bridge station.

Agarr worked fast. He opened the safes with his keys and quickly switched the lead shot for the gold bullion. By the time the train reached Redhill, where Tester was waiting, he was able to pass some of the gold to him on the station. As the train resumed its journey Agarr and Pierce continued to work quickly. They opened the boxes, transferred the contents and resealed them, and long before the train reached Folkestone the crime had been committed; the gold was in the carpet bags and the lead shot was in the boxes. All traces of anything having happened to disturb the routine had gone – and so had the gold!

When the train arrived at Folkestone the safes were manhandled out of the train. Agarr and Pierce stayed in the train until it arrived in Dover, then they collected their bags, even allowing a porter to help them carry them out of the station. They then made a leisurely journey back to London. The safes, meanwhile, were taken aboard the Channel steamer *Lord Warden*, and the ship sailed for Boulogne. Some time after it arrived there, the safes were opened with the Captain's duplicate keys as the system allowed; they were checked, weighed and put on the express for Paris. Imagine, then, the scene when the boxes were opened! As if by some mysterious means the gold had been turned into lead shot!

The investigation spread over the route from London to Paris and taxed the brains of the civil and railway police. No stone was left unturned, and someone's head would have to roll to satisfy the public for allowing this glaring crime to occur. The French authorities blamed the British and vice versa. As a matter of routine Guard Burgess was questioned, but of course he pleaded ignorance of anything untoward occurring. All railway staff along the rail route were questioned, but nobody could help. The robbery had been so well planned and executed that the authorities were without feasible clues.

Six months later the claims by the bullion merchants were met in full. The gold had gone. Rewards were offered for any news that might throw light on the theft, and many false theories were pursued, but all were found to be without foundation.

Some time after the robbery the four perpetrators met at Agarr's home in Cambridge Villas, Shepherds Bush, where for days Agarr and Pierce had melted down the bullion in a furnace; some of it was buried under the kitchen floor. Fanny Kay, a young woman who was living with Agarr, became suspicious of the hammering that emanated from the back room, but she was placated when Agarr told her that they were making 'leather aprons' and the weaving had to be hammered. Arrangements were concluded as to the share of the spoil between the four accomplices, and the charming Mr Tester was offered a very good post as General Manager of the Royal Swedish Railways, which afforded a very handsome salary. He was also in receipt of glowing references from the South Eastern Railway. Burgess stayed on the railway as a guard and Pierce disappeared into London's underworld.

Agarr, however, became rather careless. Not content with the company of Fanny Kay, he took up with another young girl, much to the anger of her regular boyfriend, named Humphreys. The latter went after Agarr over a forged cheque, which was a very serious crime in those days, and Agarr was taken to court. He was found guilty and sentenced to transportation to Australia for life.

He was a rare mix of a man – he had left his lover Fanny Kay for the other girl, yet he made provision for the child that he had sired with Fanny. While in prison he arranged with Pierce to pay Fanny regular amounts of money to help her. Pierce, however, welshed on the arrangements and none of the money ever reached the girl. Fanny, now frantic with worry, decided to take drastic action – she went to see the Governor of Newgate Prison and as a result of her evidence Agarr was brought ashore from the transport that was about to take him to Australia and made a full confession to the police, mainly, it was suspected, to get his own back on Pierce who had double-crossed him over Fanny's money.

Agarr's confession helped the police considerably, and before long William Pierce and James Burgess were brought in, and Tester was picked up as he came over from Sweden to see his family. The trial lasted three days, with Fanny Kay and Edward Agarr the principal witnesses for the Crown. Burgess and Tester were sentenced to 14 years transportation, Pierce, despite his complete disregard for poor Fanny and his previous record of felonies, was very lucky – he only received 2 years in jail. No sign of justice there!

The only money ever recovered was the sum of £2,300 in Turkish Bonds found buried under Pierce's front door step. This money became the subject of many claims, from the Crown, the City of London, the South Eastern Railway Company and Pierce's solicitor. In the end a major part of the money was allowed to the South Eastern Railway Company and the remainder to the Chief Commissioner of Police to apply it for the benefit of Fanny Kay and her child.

So ended an audacious crime, simple in its well-though-out methods and operated by intelligent people, but it failed because of one man's desire for another woman's happiness.

9

The Irish Mail train robbery

*I*n 1934 the 7.55 pm departure from Paddington was the best regular Great Western boat train. The service had begun in 1906, when the new Fishguard to Rosslare route replaced the alternative sailings from Milford Haven; it then left Paddington at 8.30 pm, stopped only at Didcot (to serve connections from the north) and Newport, and reached Fishguard in 5½ hours. Brunel is said to have estimated a 5-hour journey from Paddington to Fishguard when the route was first planned in the 1850s, and by 1909 specials had done the journey in Brunel's estimated timings.

The mail express ran until 1916, then was suspended owing to the war. It was restored in 1919, but then stopped at Reading instead of Didcot, and took 10 minutes longer to Fishguard. Nonetheless it was one of the best South Wales expresses, especially after accelerations as far as Cardiff in 1922; in that year it was suspended beyond Swansea owing to the Irish troubles, but was reintroduced in September 1923. From July 1924 the express left Paddington at 7.55 pm, as all the South Wales expresses left at 55 minutes past the hour. In 1927-28, despite diversions into and out of Swansea station instead of detaching the Swansea portion at Landore, it took only 5 hours 28 minutes throughout, but this timing was regarded as 'rather stiff'. In 1983 the journey took as long as 5 hours 47 minutes, and in the early days the train loadings were very heavy.

From 1906 the train always included a sleeping car, and from 1928 there was a 3rd Class vehicle with upper and lower berths; sometimes there was a 'support car', and from 1923 there was a carriage for Bristol Temple Meads, which was detached at Clifton Junction (where Bristol Parkway is now situated).

The South Wales and Irish mail was carried in a large 'Ocean Mail' van, so-called as the vans were often used for the conveyance of mail from the passenger liners that would lay off Plymouth and, up to 1914, Fishguard. By careful observation a criminal gang had discovered that the mail van was kept locked between stations, but that no railwaymen or Post Office staff were in it, as would have been the case on a 'Travelling Post Office' mail train.

One day in April 1934 two men appeared on No 1 platform at Paddington a few minutes before the express was due to leave, asking if a large laundry basket, a similarly large trunk and a small parcel marked 'Fragile' could be put in the mail van. They said that they did not mind how much it cost, as the conveyance of these items was very urgent; they also said that friends would meet the train at Reading and collect the luggage.

The platform staff agreed to accept the items and put them in the mail van, placing the small fragile parcel on top of the laundry basket so that nothing else would be loaded on to it. They noticed that the basket felt heavy and the trunk rather light. The express duly reached Reading punctually in 40 minutes, and sure enough two men appeared, saying that they were expecting the luggage as described. The railway staff unloaded it for them, noticing that the trunk felt heavy, and helped to load it on to a lorry. After a while the two men who had brought the luggage to Paddington arrived in a car, then the car and the lorry went off together to a quiet lane near Twyford, where they stopped and unloaded the basket and trunk. The basket lid was released and a man climbed stiffly out. What had occurred was that this man had been loaded on to the train in the basket, had got out during the journey, picked up as many registered letters and parcels as he could handle, and had got back into the basket after stuffing the loot into the trunk.

The gang told the lorry driver to drive away and make himself scarce, then they started to sort out the booty, laying it out on the grass at the side of the lane. However, they were disturbed by a courting couple out walking, panicked and drove away, leaving the stolen property where it lay. The young couple were amazed to see the ripped-open packets and parcels scattered all over the verge, realised that they had disturbed a gang of thieves and promptly informed the police.

Back at Reading, railway staff were puzzled to find very little mail in the van (which they ought to have spotted as they unloaded the laundry basket and the trunk!). They, too, realised that something was wrong, and hurriedly rang the Railway Police.

Meanwhile, the gang were making their getaway in the lorry, speeding along the main road to Maidenhead. They were going so fast and driving in such an erratic manner that quite a few people noticed their progress with alarm. Eventually an innocent motorist, driving along in a sedate manner, got in the way of the speeding lorry and there was a collision. As a result two of the gang sustained injuries, but not daring to go to the local hospital for treatment they went into a nearby public house to ask if the landlord had any bandages that they could use.

The Maidenhead police had heard about the motor accident, and put two and two together, associating the incident with the strange occurrence of the missing mail. Police arrived at the pub after being told that the gang were in the area, and apprehended and cautioned them.

One of the gang said, 'We came down to Maidenhead to see some pals. We were talking to some girls when some other blokes turned up and a disagreement occurred, then a fight started and that's how we came about these injuries.'

This was a likely tale that the police felt disinclined to believe; the men were duly arrested and charged with stealing the mail. One of the three was a well-known bookmaker, who had previously been convicted of some minor offence but had been acquitted. Two others were stage photographers, very similar in personal appearance, and they had met the lorry driver in a pub, persuading him after some conversation to drive the lorry that they had hired. He was subsequently traced and arrested, whereupon he admitted driving the lorry to and from Reading. He said that he did not realise that any criminal activity was happening, and his two 'employers' denied any knowledge of robbing the mail van – they maintained that they were quite innocent people who were driving down the lane when they saw the packets and parcels lying on the grass verge. Naturally they stopped and got out to examine the litter of registered post, and they had considered going to the police to give information, but then had the unfortunate crash.

Nonetheless, all three were brought before the Magistrate's Court at Wokingham, and the Post Office was brought into the prosecution – after all, it was their responsibility to see that the mail was handled safely and efficiently. The lorry driver made a fresh statement denying that he had seen one of the others get out of the basket. It was the usual situation – 'I never said that . . . the police made me say that . . .', and other statements wherein he either denied or changed his story. He was clearly going to be very unpredictable when his turn came to be cross-examined. However, things became rather interesting when a prosecution witness said that he had overheard the driver say, in what seemed a very suspicious conversation at the depot where he was based, that he was actually drawing his unemployment benefit at a Labour Exchange a long way away.

The three men were found guilty and were sentenced to terms of imprisonment for stealing the 'King's Mail'. Their method of concealing a man in a box, trunk or basket had been used on other occasions to steal valuables conveyed by rail, and it certainly was not to be the last time that thieves conspired to relieve the railway company of items of value by hiding in a large box locked in a mail or guard's van. But in 1934 the pace of life was different, and the sight of a lorry being driven in a reckless, erratic manner would be noticed by many more people going about their daily pursuits; the police would have been alerted by a public-spirited passer-by and the familiar Wolseley police car would proceed with all haste to the scene of the crime. The apparently lax attitude displayed by the railway staff at Paddington and Reading was, perhaps, also redolent of the attitude of the time. Certainly people were more trusting, and they believed in the complete integrity of the railway company to deliver passengers and goods intact and in good condition; the more lawless members of the community exploited the public's trust to good effect and helped themselves.

So the audacious plans of the three thieves failed. The idea could have worked but for circumstances beyond the control of the law-breakers, but perhaps not enough planning or 'fine-tuning' had been employed. In those days life in prison was pretty grim, as our three crooks, bunglers that they were, were soon to discover. . .

With acknowledgements to J. F. Wrottesley, a former lawyer involved in the case, who supplied the details.

10
The good life and the clerk

*T*his story reminds us that railway robbery does not have to be as dramatic and perhaps glamorous as thefts from the trains themselves.

Mr Edmund Denison, on the occasion of the 20th half yearly meeting of the Great Northern Railway shareholders on 23 August 1856, spoke in glowing terms of the fine state of health that the company was in at that date, and spoke of 'sound value of the property, prospects for the future excellent, the excellence and integrity of the Staff. He did not believe that there was a dishonest member of the Company; the Shareholders are being looked after very well indeed.' He finished his speech as Chairman of the company with these words: 'The line shall be well worked'.

So spoke a senior official of the well-respected Great Northern Railway in his characteristic forthright manner. But although he sounded sincere, he knew that matters were far from correct, because he had been told in the previous January that a 'discrepancy' had been found between the books of registration and the Accountant's department, and he knew that an inquiry into the supposed errors was in hand. Apparently Mr W. H. Clark, the then Chief Registrar, had been told that there was a 'trifling discrepancy', on the side of excess, between the amounts paid in dividend and the amount due to be paid on the registered stock, and according to his (Mr Clark's) statement, he had lost no time in taking necessary steps to investigate the matter and probe where the error lay.

The error lay fair and square in the lap of Mr Leopold Redpath, who was appointed on the retirement of Mr Clark to the post of Chief Registrar. Redpath had served under Mr Clark as Chief Clerk for some years. He was a man in his mid-40s, fairly tall, losing his hair at the temples but sprouting a profuse beard on his pointed chin. His work gave the impression of 'quiet efficiency', but in fact he had been systematically robbing the Great Northern Railway Company of more than £120,000, which was a lot of money in 1854! Even more staggering was the fact that he was allowed to continue in his position of trust for more than two years *after* the discrepancy had been discovered, and during those two final years he managed to lift a further £80,000 or so before his crime was discovered.

Redpath had failed in business as a wine broker, but had entered the employ of the Great Northern with good credentials. I wonder whether they were genuine? Nobody seemed to notice that his life style became one of considerable affluence considering his wage was only £250 per year. It transpired that he had bought a fine town mansion in the fashionable Regent's Park district of London, No 27 Chester Terrace, but he had left his former home in Dartmouth Terrace, Blackheath, for not paying the rent. He also bought in 1854 an equally imposing country residence by the Thames at Weybridge, he paid his cook £30 per year, he had a courier to look after him on his journeys and a fisherman and a punt for sporting excursions on the river; he also employed other servants, gave expensive dinners and receptions to the upper classes, and his apparent respect for the arts and culture placed him in high esteem by the rich whom he cultivated, explaining his affluence as being due to his expert manipulation of the Stock Exchange where he had made several good investments.

This smoke screen had enabled him to fool most of the people most of the time, but it is astonishing how easily a man might lead a double existence in a big city. He would contribute lavishly to charities and was appointed to the Board of Christ's Hospital. He travelled widely abroad and sought to collect antiques and pictures; in fact, it is said that he once out-bid Napoleon III for a painting!

The time around the mid-1850s was indeed great for speculators, but Redpath was not speculating – he was appropriating money from his employers on a colossal scale. His former boss, Mr Clark, admitted that he had very little knowledge of bookkeeping or the registration side of the company – he simply left everything to Redpath, whose knowledge of this part of the business was total.

Redpath had been creating fictitious stock and was converting it into hard cash through various brokers. He would sign fictitious names where necessary to complete the appropriate forms, and it was estimated that between his first illegitimate sale of shares in the summer of 1848 and October of 1856 he had made at least 365 sales of Great Northern stock realising the grand total of £206,000.

Eventually the fraud was exposed as the Registrar's Department was not happy about the accounts and the way that monies could not be accounted for. Redpath was summoned to meet the Chairman, who told him that the Board regarded the situation as extremely grave, and he demanded that Redpath institute a full inquiry. As the truth gradually began to emerge, Leopold Redpath decided that enough was enough, packed his bags and fled to Paris. However, for some strange reason he decided to return to face the music, and he even sent a telegram to King's Cross to inform them of his impending return.

Meanwhile the Superintendent of the Great Northern Railway police had obtained a warrant for his arrest and had planned to follow him to Paris and apprehend him there; the telegram, it was felt, was merely a ploy to put them off the scent. Nonetheless Redpath did arrive back in England, and on 14 November the police paid him a call and found him enjoying a full breakfast. He was surprised at the number of police sent to take him into custody.

The next day saw him at Clerkenwell Police Court together with a clerk who was accused of collaborating with him to defraud the GNR. The mess that Redpath had created with his manipulations of the accounts was considerable, and the prosecution had to find cases that would represent the main charges.

On 16 January 1857 Leopold Redpath stood trial at the Central Criminal Court. He was composed, even cocksure, and did not seem aware of the magnitude of the charges against him; the weight of evidence was overwhelming and the jury found him guilty. He was sentenced to transportation to Australia for life, but the clerk who was accused of being an accomplice was found not guilty and got his job back with the company.

However, the colossal mess that Redpath left took an awful lot of time to sort out, and a firm of accountants had to be called in at the cost of £100 per day. This unwanted expense could have bankrupted any other lesser firm. In the end it needed an Act of Parliament to clear up the entanglement, and the losses had to be met by the ordinary shareholders going without their half-year dividend. The GNR had to purchase the stock, then cancel all the illegal shares. The final bill for this catastrophic fraud was more than £250,000, of which only £25,000 was available from the sale of Redpath's goods and chattels. So the fraud that Leopold Redpath so cleverly contrived nearly bankrupted the Great Northern Railway Company, and the ripples took a long and costly time to reach the shore, required an inordinate amount of time and shareholders money to unravel, and serves as a caution to others bent on fleecing the firms for whom they work. It's not worth it!

11
The ticket fraud

Mr William Dunn lived at Shortwood House, Staines, Middlesex. One July day in 1854 he purchased a ticket to travel from Staines to London on the South Western Railway, returning in the evening. He was known in the district as an honourable gentleman and above any reproach, so as his reputation was impeccable and well-known the South Western Railway's employees at Staines station greeted him respectfully, took a cursory glance at his ticket and opened the door of a 1st Class compartment for him. At one time Mr Dunn was a regular season ticket holder and no one would believe that his habits would change for the worst. But he exploited this trust of his personal reputation to good effect by using the same daily return ticket for nearly two years.

However, all good things come to an inevitable end and one day the train stopped at Mortlake and the Station Master, as a matter of routine, asked to see Mr Dunn's ticket. He produced a ticket and was about to return it to his pocket when the eagle-eyed official asked if he could examine it. Then a strange thing happened – Mr Dunn was seized with an uncontrolled desire to visit the water closet, and remained there for a considerable time.

The Station Master obviously had had some experience of this kind of situation before and waited patiently. He guessed that Mr Dunn was attempting to alter the ticket somehow, and he was interested to see if he would bluff it out and try to get on the train amid the bustle and movement of the other travellers as they boarded and alighted. Mr Dunn appeared from the water closet looking very uncomfortable – he knew that he had been found out.

The official snatched the ticket, put on his spectacles and studied the piece of paste-board. It had been altered, and not very well; Mr Dunn had obviously tried, clumsily, to change the figure '4' into a '6'.

Here was a man of supposed substance and integrity stooping to a shabby trick of trying to avoid pay his train fare. The South Western Railway company obtained a summons and this was served in person; Mr Dunn had to attend court and either defend or deny the action, but he stated that he did not think it proper to do so. The railway company had therefore to apply for a warrant against him. As proof of personal service of the summons had been given, the warrant was granted.

The agents of the South Western Railway attended at Lambeth Police Court to prosecute a charge of fraud upon the company by Mr William Dunn, Gentleman. They waited until 2 o'clock, and as the defendant had still not made an appearance, the case was entered upon. Mr Dunn could not make any appearance before anyone except the Almighty, because he was dead.

Shortly after the Magistrate took his seat on the bench, one of the summoning officers informed him that on Saturday evening the warrant had been placed in his hands and on going to Waterloo that morning to execute it he had learned that a man answering Mr Dunn's description had drowned himself at the Old Royal Baths in Newgate Street. The official had visited the Baths and confirmed that the body was indeed that of Mr Dunn.

Mr Dunn had ordered a private shilling bath, and a bedroom had been prepared for him. He seemed to be in the bath a long time, but the staff were used to such eccentricities and it was only when they were about to lock the place up that they found Mr Dunn drowned. On the table beside the bath was his gold watch, his spectacles, two rings and a small sum of money. From certain documents found in his pockets it was clear that he had problems beside the ticket fraud; one was a letter from a London legal firm threatening immediate legal proceedings against Mr Dunn unless £3,000 was paid.

So ends the unfortunate story of Mr William Dunn, whose unknown but desperate financial position led him to see no way out but the taking of his own life; a gentleman's high esteem tarnished by desperate events, and deciding to end his life rather than be tried ignominiously in a court.

12
Parcel pilferage

*M*any thefts are successfully executed because of the unreliable nature of the system and the quick-wittedness of people who see and take opportunities to 'cash in' on the weaknesses. The following tales were related to the author by a railway employee working in the London suburbs in the early 1960s. He worked in the goods, passenger and parcels departments dealing with all aspects of railway work.

One of his duties was to undertake the compilation of the sheets dealing with inward parcels that came from one of the London termini in the Scammell three-wheeler articulated 'mechanical horse' lorries, quaint but very practical in their day. There were three journeys per day, and the parcels were for delivery to private addresses, shops and businesses. At that time 90 per cent of parcels for private addresses were from the major mail order firms, and they had unique labels bearing letters (certain combinations signifying, for example, 'Paid home') and numbers. These numbers were entered on the delivery sheet, and when the driver delivered it he obtained a signature from the recipient which proved delivery.

Subsequently British Railways, in conjunction with the mail order firms, decided to stop using individual labels in favour of a rubber stamp with a code signifying 'Deliver to address' but no special number. This was obviously meant to save the time and costs associated with sticking and recording each label, and it was fine except that some of the agents received dozens of parcels each week, and because the delivery sheets could not differentiate between parcels, BR could not be certain if a specific parcel had been delivered if asked for proof of delivery. Certain bright but lawless agents took this heaven-sent opportunity to report parcels as missing, and BR could not prove whether if in fact this was the case. This was a situation that, if left to continue, would have cost the railways a tremendous amount of money. This apparent loophole on the system brought a record number of claims for missing parcels; the numbers soared by more than 500 per cent, and even though it was known that some of the agents were on the fiddle, it could not be proved. Even if BR wrote asking if a certain parcel had been received, invariably the reply was in the negative.

It was also suspected that some of the railway staff were removing goods en route because of the laxity of the system. It was well known that if you had a parcel to send and you addressed it correctly, you could leave it on one of the trollies full of parcels that were always around at main-line stations, and BR would happily deliver it free of charge.

Another 'crime' in conjunction with parcels was concerned with a BR lorry driver. These drivers would take out a lorry-load of parcels in the morning, returning in the evening with the empty lorry and delivery sheets full of signatures from happy recipients of their eagerly awaited parcels.

It was not long before a lot of 'Proofs of Delivery' were required from one area, and it was discovered that this driver had a married girlfriend in the area, so only delivered about half of the parcels, dumping the rest in a large pond in the locality. The driver admitted this after being followed one day by the British Transport Police and BR's Commercial Manager. When the pond was dragged over 100 parcels were dredged up, by this time in a terrible condition, but they still had to be delivered with the result that still more claims came flooding in.

BR also had offices in London's dockland. To get into the Docks from Custom House station or from the main road meant that dockers and BR staff had to walk over a long footbridge that had a police hut on it. If anyone had any valuables about their person, such as cameras, radios, watches or jewellery, they had to sign a book to say that they were taking them in, and when they left work in the evening they had to sign the book again to get their property back. Unfortunately old box Brownies and old watches were taken in and brand new SLR cameras and Rolex and Omega watches were taken out without the police suspecting anything until one day a particularly bright officer questioned a number of people, who were subsequently prosecuted.

Many of the dockers travelled to Stratford from Custom House station, and they would dash down the stairs at the last minute, telling the station staff that they would pay at Stratford. When they arrived at Stratford, however, one docker would offer a £10 note to the sole member of the barrier staff, usually querying the fare and checking his change; meanwhile his mates would pass through the barrier without paying. In those days nobody dared challenge the dockers, usually because they were generally bigger than the staff and their size enabled them to get away with most things.

In the docks large amounts of driftwood and damaged packing cases were collected and bundled together as firewood, and sent by rail on behalf of the 'poor' dockers to their home addresses. This went on for some time until a bundle of wood was 'dropped' and split open to reveal an interesting collection of expensive watches; further investigations of other bundles brought to light parcels of tobacco, cameras, more foreign watches and some very fascinating foreign glossy magazines, the contents of which would make most people's hair stand on end!

At Poplar Docks other illegal activities occurred. There used to be a considerable traffic in export whisky brought down from Scotland in sealed 'Vanfit' wagons, and consigned through Millwall Docks to America and sometimes European destinations. On a number of occasions the wagons were opened to find a partially loaded or empty wagon. Although the seals were still intact, part of the floor was missing; what had happened in the various marshalling yards en route was that the thieves had got underneath the wagon, sawn through the floor and 'lifted' the goods. The British Transport Police followed the consignments but did not catch many thieves; no doubt they had been tipped off!

One other dodge that seemed to be successful was the free whisky that was obtained as a result of 'accidents' when a large – often *very* large – bottle was unfortunately 'dropped'. It was quite amazing to see the appearance of bottles of all sizes that emerged from some people's pockets and 'snap-boxes', so evidently most of the 'spillage' was not wasted!

In Poplar Docks ships and barges were unloaded, and the light-fingered brigade were very active there too. One item of traffic was copper bars, destined for the Pirelli Rubber Company at their works on the Southern Region. On one occasion a car belonging to one of the unloading staff was seen by the railway police crawling along with the rear of the car scraping along the road with sparks flying. Needless to say, when the police stopped the car and, in the course of investigation, opened the boot, a weighty cargo of copper bars was discovered. . .

13
Operation Antler

*T*his is the story of the downfall of a man who had devoted a very useful life as a reliable, loyal servant of his firm; indeed, he had received a gold watch for 25 years of faithful service. But in his retirement he turned to crime, and in the space of no more than two years more than 500 complaints were received concerning his nefarious activities. Losses of luggage, including briefcases, suitcases, holdalls and other items, literally stolen from the racks of trains on the King's Cross to Edinburgh East Coast route, increased alarmingly, and the British Transport Police thought that they were dealing with a highly organised gang. The amount of money that the items represented was in excess of £200,000, and the police held a top-level meeting at King's Cross to discuss ways and means of solving this growing crime.

The result was the setting up of a secret divisional investigation, code-named 'Operation Antler' (after the famous brand of hand luggage). A team of four officers travelled on the trains, clocking up more than 48,000 miles between them.

'At first we didn't know exactly what we were looking for, and when we started we had nothing to go on. There was no obvious pattern because none of the victims knew exactly where their luggage had been stolen,' explained a member of the team. It was going to be a long job.

Two officers travelled on southbound trains while the other two took the northbound services. In each train an apparently scruffy, unshaven character squatted on the matting of the vestibules near the toilets to keep an eye on movements of passengers, while his partner sat in a comfortable seat watching the luggage racks inside the carriage. As they had nothing to work on the initial methods were to gather information and carry out general surveillance.

A data-base was created at York station, for which a special computer program was written. Details of all the thefts were fed into the computer, and it announced that they were all taking place between York and Edinburgh, and shortly it had managed to narrow the field down to between York and Newcastle. It then identified the carriage – all the stolen suitcases were from Coach D. Finally it even came up with the day of the thefts, Wednesday.

Consequently the officers moved permanently into Coach D, but in time the pattern changed, and the suitcases were being lifted from Coach C. So the officers changed their seating again. They kept in touch with each other by secret equipment and every Thursday they had a meeting with their team leader at York, where they exchanged information.

One day a man stepped on to a northbound train at Darlington. He was carrying a holdall and, noticing the scruffy man sitting on the floor in the vestibule, he told the unfortunate fellow of a vacant seat in Coach C. A few minutes later another man joined the first and they got off at Newcastle. The police officer made a mental note of the luggage they were carrying, and on arrival at Edinburgh the two officers hurried to the BTP office. Sure enough a lady came in to report the loss of her luggage – the same luggage that the policeman had seen the two men with when they left the train at Newcastle. Now the team had some substantial information and they felt confident that it was only a matter of time before they would have their man.

A few weeks later fortune smiled on them again, as once more the same man stepped aboard the train, but this time he had reversed his journey, catching a southbound service at Newcastle. As the officer later reported, 'The man I had seen on the previous occasion sat opposite me, but he didn't recognise the unshaven creature that he nearly fell over in the vestibule. Ten minutes from Darlington he took a suitcase from the rack and took it to the door at the end of the coach, then he came back to his seat. He still didn't know me, and when the train stopped he picked up the luggage as he got out.'

That was the end of the line for the thief, as two large policemen were waiting for him to give up his stolen luggage. In his blue holdall they found keys capable of opening suitcases and a ring and other jewellery belonging to a passenger who had reported the theft at York. The man was questioned for a long time at York, and when the police searched his home they found a robber's den. There were chemicals and equipment for testing the quality of gold, silver and platinum, scales for weighing precious metals, and lists of gold prices and the latest dealer's charges for trading in bullion. They also found many skeleton keys and timetables for trains between Darlington, Edinburgh, Newcastle and King's Cross. But they did not finish there. A further search revealed £34,000 worth of bonds, £20,000 in the thief's name and £14,000 in the name of a young teenage relation.

At the trial, the Defence explained that these bonds came from the accused's investments, including the sale of his father's house, while other money came from long-term investments and money on deposit at high interest. The accused had four bank accounts, all in his name but with different banks in different towns. He had even reported the theft of his own luggage, not once but three times, and each claim had been paid out by the insurance company. He claimed for the loss of his gold retirement watch, his spectacles, his electric shaver, false teeth and rare pigeon annuals, and had been paid more than £2,300 without raising suspicion.

What actually caused his downfall was greed, as with so many criminals before him. His sentence was comparatively light: he received 18 months for theft, three months to run concurrently for deception, and was ordered to pay compensation and costs. However, 12 months of his sentence was suspended after he pleaded guilty to nine charges of theft and deception involving property worth more than £8,000. He had been prepared to plead not guilty until an hour before the trial began, but the overwhelming evidence of the discovery of the stolen goods at his home and the equally damning evidence rolled out by the computer finally convinced him that he was left to the mercy of the court.

And following his arrest there was a marked drop in thefts of luggage on the East Coast Main Line.

14
The affair at Calton Loop

A century after those first daring train robberies, theft from trains was still rife on our railways, and still providing a headache for the stretched resources of the railway police. One case of bravery and dedication that deserves space in this book is the round-up of a gang that was alleged to have robbed goods trains and taken many thousands of pounds worth of goods of all kinds. Their sheer determination and complete disregard for law and order made this gang very dangerous; if caught in the act of robbery, there was no doubt that they would even kill to get away, and on this particular occasion it is only by luck and the fitness of the constables concerned that they survived the vicious attack by these desperate men.

In the 1950s a series of robberies had occurred in the Doncaster area and strenuous attempts had been made by the railway police to apprehend the gang. On one occasion the police had sprung a trap on the villains, only for them to escape, knocking out a police dog in the process. It became obvious that strong measures would have to be employed to bring these men to justice, and special observation was called for. At one time about 25 railway policemen were involved in surveillance at selected spots, and as many as 4,000 hours were spent trying to prevent further crimes – but each time the gang got away.

After much deliberation and planning, the railway police decided to stake out an area near Calton Loop, between Doncaster and Newark. Accordingly one September night three constables in plain clothes, Metcalfe, Cook and Norton, were watching the loop from a nearby field. Shortly after midnight they saw a Doncaster-bound goods train pull into the loop. When it stopped they saw lights moving about and the sounds of parcel van doors being opened, followed by packages being thrown to the ground.

The three policemen ran towards the train thinking that this was the chance that they had been waiting for. One of the thieves ran towards the signal box and got away, but another was tackled in a lane near the line; however, his calls for help resulted in three other villains appearing. The resulting fight was nasty – the robbers were vicious, and it is only by a miracle that Constable Norton was not killed by the savage attack. One of the gang attacked Norton with a steel hook on the end of a rope, which embedded itself into Norton's skull. As if he was not badly injured enough, one of the gang then smashed him on the back of the head with his own truncheon.

Meanwhile Constable Metcalfe was not doing much better. He had been knocked out by one of the gang using a stick filled with lead, known to have been used by the gang leader. Constable Cook had also suffered serious head injuries. After rendering the three policemen powerless, the gang escaped.

It is a wonder that Constable Norton survived with his life; he had lost a lot of blood, but he managed to stagger a mile to the nearest police station. He looked so bad that when the local Sergeant's daughter saw him she fainted. Cook and Metcalfe managed to find a crossing-keeper's cottage, and a short time afterwards Cook found Norton at the police station and was able to render first aid to such effect that he was awarded the meritorious First Aid Certificate for his skill in treating his colleague.

The police were now determined to bring this vicious gang to justice, and they stepped up their surveillance and enquiries. They had long suspected the man known to be the gang leader, and knew that he was involved in the robberies, but they had to have conclusive proof. This man had a bad criminal record and had had numerous previous convictions for robbery and assault, stealing from railway property, and had resisted arrest on occasions.He was also a poacher, and knew all the tricks. His house was therefore placed under surveillance to see just what his movements were.

One day, in the early hours of the morning, the police spotted the man's son arrive home. He came out later and dug a hole in the front garden and buried what later proved to be large steel hook, a belt and a pair of bolt-croppers. The police pounced and arrested him, and after taking him to the nearest police station they returned to collect his father, who did not take very kindly to being arrested. He attempted to resist again, but this time unsuccessfully.

Another member of the gang was picked up after his fingerprints had been found on one of the packages stolen from the train, and another was arrested a few days later. All the men were identified by the three police officers. The father and son received heavy prison sentences; the Judge at their trial told the gang leader that he was a complete menace to society. The second gang member arrested also received a long prison sentence, but the jury could not agree on a decision regarding the fourth man, and he was committed for retrial.

Guarding a siding in the middle of nowhere is a tedious, boring job, but on occasions it is a vital part of the process of defeating the criminal. The real risk is in apprehending the robbers in the act, and this can be, and often is, very dangerous. There is always the chance that a gun, knife or another offensive weapon is being carried, which certain villains will not hesitate to use. These three officers were lucky to survive this particular incident.

This is not the only case mentioned in this book of policemen being badly hurt while guarding railway property. More often than not the police get their man, but spare a thought for the long hours crouched under a wagon in the dark, or waiting under a hedge in the pouring rain waiting for the opportunity to grab a villain as he breaks open a wagon and helps himself to the contents. Police dogs, too, can play a vital role in catching the criminals, and they are an important part of the modern British Railways police force.

The three officers recovered from their terrible injuries and returned to duty; they all received commendations from Sir Brian Robertson, Chairman of the British Transport Commission, for their bravery and dedication to duty.

15
The joy-riders

*F*inally, from theft from trains to what can only be described as theft *of* trains! One would imagine it impossible to operate a complex mass of diesel-electric machinery with a very basic item of household equipment like a spoon. But this was proved to be the case in an incident when a 16-year-old boy actually started and ran a main-line diesel-electric locomotive a distance of some 10 miles; the fact that three other teenagers took it in turn to drive the engine makes the events seem even more incredible, but it happened.

The boys will no doubt never forget their experience, although it will be tarnished by the fact that they were caught and punished for their misdemeanours. The escapade started, as they usually do, with curiosity, then the desire to emulate the 'grown-ups'; unfortunately the one important factor missing was experience and knowledge of the machine and railway system procedures. But bravado was going to make up for that. We must remember that a qualified locomotive driver goes through a most comprehensive and rigorous 27-week training course that includes all aspects of the job before they can take any locomotive out on to the main line. Amongst his essential kit every driver has his master key that unlocks the driving controls in the cab.

The boys' local line was mainly used for coal traffic in connection with local collieries, and the nearby BR Motive Power Depot looked after the locomotives required. The depot had 'holding' sidings and a marshalling yard consisting of up and down sidings; the signal box controlling the movements for the depot was to be found at the up sidings.

The main offenders in this sequence of events were two 16-year-old boys, but also involved were an 18-year-old and another boy of 17, together with others as young as 12 and 15. They were ostensibly trainspotters, almost fanatical, and they regularly travelled all over the country in pursuit of their hobby. It all started when one of the 16-year-olds in his many visits to the depot found his interest moving from taking numbers to actually climbing aboard the many engines stabled in the holding sidings. He would gaze at the array of controls and sit in the driver's seat imagining that he was in control of the engine, and soon the idea entered his head that it might be possible to try and start the engine up. He had discovered that the master key was essential to unlock the driving controls and had tried unsuccessfully to break the lock with a screwdriver and a knife handle. Give him full marks for sheer persistence – one day he arrived with a spoon, which with some effort he bent and inserted in the lock. Hey presto! He could now start the engine.

Quite frankly he did not think anyone would believe that he had started a locomotive with a twisted spoon! But he could not keep the fact to himself, and told a friend all about it. They were so excited that he took his pal back to the sidings and showed him how it was done; the other boy was most impressed and they then tried to move the engine to have a run up the sidings, but on this occasion were unable to master the controls. Such was their determination, however, that they returned on at least seven occasions to try to get the engine moving, and at last by design or accident the big locomotive started to move. The boys were delighted – they drove up and down the siding, they were in control, and their egos were growing fast!

Soon, of course, their fellow spotters heard about their triumph and some turned up at the depot to see the fun. Of course the next step was to drive the locomotive on the main line; they presumably gave no thought to the potential danger involved. A lot of talk and planning was now afoot and the boys decided that their plan was to unlock the points to the main line and drive a locomotive along the line and back. This would be a real challenge to their ingenuity, but the ease with which they achieved this bold and highly dangerous escapade was frightening.

The plan needed clear minds and logic, and at 16 the boys had plenty of that. They would have to get into the signal box and pull the right lever to obtain access to the main line, and in order to do that they had to get into the box and have a good look around to see just what was involved. They therefore decided to break in. On arriving at the box they found a window open, so climbed in and found the point levers. Now all was set up for the adventure of a lifetime.

The boys decided on the time of their feat and planned to drive one of the locomotives that were usually stabled in the sidings on to the main line and travel to the next town and back. One thing they had to check on was whether there were any 'catch points' in the line, as these faced the 'wrong' way on a running line to catch and derail any part of a runaway train that was running back. They therefore walked the line to satisfy themselves that there were none; there would then seem to be no reason why the adventure could not go ahead. They had got quite a lot of practice driving the locomotives up and down the sidings – nobody saw them and access was easy. The spoon was always available, so starting was not a problem.

One Saturday afternoon the two 16-year-olds and a friend two years older entered the depot and found their chosen locomotive parked in the sidings; it was there for the weekend. They forced a window in the signal box and moved two levers to operate the main-line points; they then changed the hand-operated points and checked that all was clear to move the engine on to the main line.

Returning to the loco, they used the spoon to unlock the mechanism and started the engines; they roared into life and the boys were ready to go. They slowly drove along the sidings out on to the main line and over a level crossing; the automatic barriers were working normally and were in the 'down' position across the road as the loco passed. One of the 16-year-olds drove the engine, travelling at speeds varying between 20 and 40 mph.

When they reached their intended destination the driver decided to go on to the next town, where he stopped, and his friend took over to drive back. When they reached the level crossing they noticed that the half barriers stayed down after their passage; this was because they were travelling along the line in the wrong direction. The 18-year-old climbed down and tried to move the barriers, but they were locked, so they carried on back to the depot, parked the loco in its siding, replaced the points and went home highly satisfied!

As in a lot of cases in life, the stable door is locked after the horse has bolted; in this case the railway police were called to the level crossing to investigate why the barriers appeared to be stuck and the red lights flashing, holding up road traffic. It was rather a mystery, because as far as they knew no trains had been on the line. A technician was sent to repair the fault and try to find out what had caused it; he soon effected the repair and road traffic returned to normal.

When the signalman discovered that one of the windows in the box had been forced, he reported the fact to the railway police.

Acting on information received, the police interviewed a local boy who admitted his part in taking the locomotive, together with his two 16-year-old friends. They were also interviewed, but they denied any association with the other boy. After extensive enquiries in the area, it was revealed that the two 16-year-old boys together with another boy had driven a shunting locomotive within the depot, and also that the youth had used an adjustable spanner to start and operate the engine.

More enquiries took place and achieved some success. One of the 16-year-olds admitted that he was involved in the driving of the engines, and after searching his home the police found a considerable amount of BR property, including a BR Locomotive Operating Manual, which the boy admitted he had stolen from the cab of a locomotive. The twisted spoon was also found, and the boy admitted a great deal of information that blew the whole adventure sky high!

A couple of months later a storeman in the depot stores found that quite a lot of items of BR property had been taken, including jackets, 'high-visibility' vests, a pair of trousers and a cap. Despite these investigations, the boys' fun continued. A diesel shunter was parked for the weekend in the sidings, and a local resident saw it being driven backwards and forwards along the sidings. A number of youths were seen in the cab, and were later identified as the 18-year-old and the two 16-year-olds; incredibly one of them had started the loco by turning the master switch by hand. The boys were dressed in the railway uniforms that had been stolen from the stores. Later that evening the same three were 'engine drivers' of two types of main-line diesel locos up and down the holding sidings; they stopped and picked up younger children along the track to give them 'joy rides'.

The youths were rounded up, brought to court and charged with entering railway property and using means to effect entry to locomotives, starting up engines and driving them, and stealing railway property. To prove the point a Traction Inspector successfully started a loco with the very spoon that had been used by the boys, and admitted that the Operating Manual would have been of great help to the offenders in understanding and operating the engines.

The defendants pleaded guilty to some of the charges and not guilty to others. In spite of the severity of the charges and the potential danger to the public that might have ensued, not to mention the danger to themselves, their punishment was comparatively, perhaps ridiculously, light, involving modest fines and amounts of compensation to BR.

It seems quite astonishing that such events could have been allowed to happen. We as a nation are so trusting, and the most incredible situations can occur under our noses. The boys concerned regarded the whole affair as one big adventure; they gave little or no thought to their own safety or that of anyone else. They simply found themselves in a wonderland of locomotives and rolling-stock, discovered that they could play with them, and their ingenuity enabled some of them to drive the engines without any thought of the consequences. Thank heaven that no one was hurt, for this tale of derring-do could so easily have been one of death or serious injury.

Part Three: Grievous Bodily Harm

16
Railway riots and the navvies

*I*n the years around the early 1840s when the railways were being
hacked out of mountainsides and laid across bogs and moorland,
the mainstay of the human machine that lent its muscular effort to
the thankless job of wielding a pick-axe and swinging a shovel was
the 'navvy'. Irish, Scottish and English, their native temperaments
could not have been more diverse – the easy-going Roman
Catholic Irish, the Presbyterian Scots and the rather intolerant
English.

The Irish came peaceably enough. They built their huts and, their
ideas of comfort being very austere, their living accommodation was
rough in the extreme. However, their sense of humour and purpose
in life was that of the carefree. Until they got strong drink inside
them they would be prepared to work for modest pay, and that
arrangement tended to be applied also to the Scots and English
labourers, as the contractors wanted to spend as little as possible on
the navvies.

In general the Irish navvies tended to regard the Sabbath as a time
for lazy idleness – on the Sabbath they sang and relaxed. They also
drank. The Scots navvies also drank a lot on the Sabbath and prayed
that drink would be always available and that they would be given
strength to beat up the godless Irish. The Irish defended themselves and
much annoyed the Scots, who did not rate their Hibernian neighbours
as fighting men. The English navvies would fight anyone; but recruited
mainly from Yorkshire and Lancashire, they always preferred to beat up
the Irish!

The contractors tried to keep the warring factions apart, in
particular the Scots and Irish, using them on different parts of the line.
The Scots were bound, however, by their religious beliefs, and the Irish
offended these.

On one occasion notices were posted in towns along the line:

'That all the Irish men on the line of Railway in Fife Share must be off the grownd and out of the Countey on Monday th 11th of this month or els we must by the strenth of our armes and a good pick axe shaft put them off.

Your Humbel Servants

Schots men'

Similarly, letters were also sent to the contractors and sub-contractors:

'Sir – You must warn all your Irish men to be out of the grownd on Monday 11th of this month at 12 o clock or els we must put them by fors.

For WE
Are determined
To Dow it'

Then the Sheriff arrived and warned the now excited Scots against doing anything of a lawless nature. Two hundred navvies met on a beach but, remembering the Sheriff's warning, decided to disperse; the Irish were left to fight another day!

However, in other areas the effect of the rioting navvies was far more serious. Some 7,000 men were working on the stretch of the line through Lockerbie, and they were paid monthly in the town, usually at a pub. The trouble was getting them out of the pub and back to work, for after a good few glasses of ale they got fighting mad and no one could reason with them. On one payday a mob of about 300 attacked the few Irish who worked on the line, a bloody conflict being only just prevented by the timely arrival of a force of militia from Carlisle.

Two of the worst incidents occurred in February 1846, one at Penrith and the other at Gorebridge near Edinburgh. The trouble at Penrith started in an innocuous kind of way. An Irishman was told by an English ganger to use a shovel instead of a pick. The Irishman refused to be told anything by an Englishman, feelings were roused, one thing led to another and the English, who were in the majority, tried to drive the awkward Irish off the excavations. They burned the Irish living accommodation, which consisted of wooden huts that were crude in the extreme, and the poor Irish, together with wives and children, were turned out into a bleak Scottish winter with nowhere to find shelter.

Word soon reached other Irishmen from construction camps near

Penrith and the next day around 500 Irishmen took up their picks and shovels to get even with the English. Given prior notice of the advancing Irish horde the English fled, so when the Irish arrived at the camp no one was there. They were now tired of marching and decided to resign themselves to the fact that they had had a wasted journey, and drifted back to Penrith.

However, the English had decided to settle with the Irish at the first opportunity, and a great horde of English navvies, thirsting for a fight, advanced on Penrith intending to thrash the living daylights out of their opponents. Soon more than 2,000 English navvies had assembled in the town – but the Irish had got wind of their promised thrashing and had dispersed. However, this time there was no stopping the ranting navvies, and they ransacked the town looking for the enemy. They found around 12 of them and subjected them to extreme cruelty, beating them unconscious. One Englishman, John Hobday, beat Irishman Denis Salmon so badly that he, Hobday, was sentenced to 15 years transportation; as he was being sentenced, he turned and laughed at the Judge. In the end the Westmorland Yeomanry had to restore law and order.

Mixing the Irish with the English or Scottish was asking for trouble; the navvies had short tempers and when they had had a drink mayhem would result. Riots spread as far south as Kendal and some 50 Irishmen appealed to the Mayor of Kendal that they had been chased from the construction site by the Scots and their huts had been destroyed and pillage had occurred. The Mayor did what he could and had a handbill printed reminding 'To whom it may concern' that the peace in the area would be protected by force if necessary. The Irish returned to work, but the Mayor and his men kept a strict surveillance on the scene.

Graham Spiers, Sheriff for the Edinburgh area, was most unhappy at the lot of the navvies. He knew of the intolerable conditions that existed and he had the unenviable job of trying to keep law and order among the undisciplined rabble that was constructing the railway. Life in the construction camps was at that time almost indescribable. The sleeping huts were crude and insanitary, the food was of poor quality and often uneatable, and the work arduous in the extreme, hacking out cuttings and tunnels in all weathers. The work was done for contractors who paid the men as little as possible, and the gangers who organised the navvies were usually bullies, and indeed were often chosen for their attitude as such. They had to force many of the navvies to work, then keep at them to ensure that they kept working. In addition the men were swindled at the 'tommy shops' run by the contractors. These so-called shops sold everything, but they also ran a credit system whereby the men could obtain credit against their wages.

It is likely that the contractors were as afraid of the navvies as the navvies were afraid of the bullies, for the contractors generally had little or no control over their labourers. Fear spread fear, and the local population learned to fear the navvies, too, and were very pleased when they moved on. Many navvies were killed in the course of the back-breaking work, and the contractors were always pushing the work on as fast as possible, as they would get paid as it progressed.

The trouble at Gorebridge was the worst example of the breakdown of law and order amongst these men. The Irishmen had been paid in a pub, and some of them said they had not been paid enough – they could not read or add up, but they thought they had been 'done' by the contractor. However, although their credit at the 'tommy shop' had used up a great percentage of their wage, there was still enough to get drunk on.

Then a rather naive journeyman arrived at the pub and got talking to the Irishmen, asking them if they wanted to buy a watch. As the Irishmen could hardly tell the time, a watch was useless, but they nevertheless expressed interest and the pedlar showed them his watches, which were handed round to much nodding of heads and whispers. The pedlar then asked for the money or the watches.

The navvies looked at one another. Watches? What watches? The pedlar could see little point in arguing with drunken Irishmen, so he made his way to the local police station to complain. The law duly moved in, dragged two of the navvies out of the pub and arrested them. They were then slung into the cells for the night pending other investigations. Their colleagues did not like this turn of events and decided to go and free their mates. Armed with pick-axes, shovels and any other weapon they could find they marched on the police station.

The two men on duty, Sergeant Brown and Constable Christie, tried to placate the men, but the Irish were not having any truck with the law. They pushed the two officers out of the way and pulled the cell door down; Brown and Christie were injured in the melée and threatened with a pistol. The navvies then departed and marched off towards Fushie Bridge, but they had not gone far before they met two policemen on their rounds, District Constable Richard Pace and John Veitch of the railway police. The two officers heard the navvies' voices and, realising what might happen, hid in a hedge, but the navvies found them and beat them both unconscious. Pace was so badly injured that he later died. Fortunately Veitch survived and later gave evidence of the attack by the drunken men.

The news of the disturbance and Pace's death soon reached Edinburgh and the Sheriff decided to send a force of 24 men to Gorebridge. They reached the village by noon, but by now all was quiet. Not for long, however, for news of the trouble reached the navvies working on the line in the south; most of them were Scots and some English, and they swore revenge.

Early on the Monday morning about 1,000 navvies marched towards the Irish huts. The local policeman saw the column in the distance and sent a rider off to Edinburgh to report what was going on; a further detachment of police was sent from Edinburgh in a coach and four, and the cavalry at Piershill Barracks were warned of the situation.

By this time the column of navvies were picking up support as they marched and had been joined by about 150 colliers from the Marquess of Lothian's mines, who also hated the Irish. The force was now around 1,500 strong armed with weapons and with banners and flags flying, and a piper and bugler adding to their shouts and songs. When they reached Crichton Muir the Irish spotted this awesome and hostile horde and, deciding that discretion was the better part of valour, they fled. When the horde reached the Irish camp they went berserk. They smashed up any of the Irish possessions and burned the miserable huts, leaving behind a stinking heap of smouldering ruins. It was pitiful to see the Irish women and their sobbing children watching their possessions being destroyed by the rampaging navvies.

Sheriff Spiers arrived when it was all over. The navvies had by this time dispersed, but the next day about 200 Irishmen tried to get even with the Scots. However, they ran into Spiers and his men who soon warned them of the consequences of any attempt to break the law. The murderers had got away. Forewarned of Spiers's arrival, they had fled south. A reward of £50 was offered for the capture of the men and descriptions were issued, but the trail had gone cold and the murderers were never caught.

The navvies drank every day at their work, but the main abuse of alcohol was on paydays. The contractors were asked to pay the men weekly, but they feared that if they did so work would never get done; navvies might drink themselves unconscious on payday and it took about three days to get themselves sober enough to resume work. These drinking sessions, or 'randies', mostly occurring on or near payday, were feared in whatever part of the country a line was being constructed. The population was powerless to stop the outrages from which the navvies derived their enjoyment – poaching, hunting with packs of dogs, theft of all kinds and destruction of property.

In 1845 at Katrine on the Muirkirk and Ayr line the locals were aghast when some of the navvies lured a tinker into the local pub and got him drunk; they then stripped him of his clothes. They would also get very argumentative when drunk and were very likely to dispute their change – they would on occasions threaten to wreck the pub if the landlord crossed them. The landlords did not want them in any case, and cursed the railway for wanting to build a line in the area!

The 'randies' would envelope many kinds of entertainment besides drinking and poaching. Prize-fighting became popular and grudge matches were arranged, the matches being fought until one or both men became senseless or one died as the result of the beating he suffered; these fights were protracted and very gory. In many cases the local landowners were powerless to stop the indiscriminate poaching on their land, as gangs of navvies accompanied by dogs and armed with shot-guns would roam over growing crops shooting at anything that moved.

If the navvies could not find a pub in the area, they would take to making their own beer, which they would sell without a licence. This meant that the men were drunk most of the time and no work was being done. The home-made ale was extremely strong and its effect on the men was frightening. The contractors were very worried about the illicit beer and on one occasion when they found the source of the home brew they locked the barrels up in a wooden building. The men decided that they could not do without their beer and they broke down the door and found the barrels. A free-for-all ensued during which they managed to drink the barrels dry. This led to the inevitable fight, and the inhabitants of the nearby village of Wescoe Hill were terrified to witness the cruelty and dreadful noise of the men fighting each other for no apparent reason.

The navvies had gone into a grass field to fight their drunken feuds and when they had finally tired of the 'randy' they staggered out of the nearly flattened field leaving one man dead, lying on a pile of stones. He had, of course, been drinking with his mates and had indulged in the drunken brawls, but things had got out of hand, and in the alcoholic haze that enveloped most of the combatants he was singled out for amusement. He was stripped naked, water was thrown at him again and again, then he was beaten up, covered in soot then drenched again with water. The effect of his savage treatment must have resulted in death.

The actual work of building the railway was carried out amidst continuing feuds. Men were set against each other and often fights would break out during the course of a day's work. 'Accidents' would happen when the ganger's back was turned, and often death resulted, but the assailant would never be found. Nevertheless the navvy's loyalty took strange forms in those far-off days, and the so-called Battle of Mickleton was an example of what could happen between builders and navvies when different circumstances arose.

Mickleton was a village on the course of the Oxford, Worcester &

Wolverhampton Railway, and the line was being laid by navvies employed indirectly by the great railway engineer Isambard Kingdom Brunel himself. However, work was progressing far too slowly and Brunel, the engineer appointed to oversee the construction, had to appoint another contractor who would hopefully speed the job along. But still the work ground on very slowly and Brunel was not pleased – he suspended the contractor and sent for a man named Marchant, instructing him to get things moving with no further delay. However, still disputes and stoppages of all kinds, mainly over the terms of the contract, dogged the progress of the line. The building of Mickleton Tunnel was the main bone of contention.

The railway company had had enough of the delays and disputes, and decided to take possession of the works. It handed over the contract to Messrs Peto & Betts, who were responsible for constructing the rest of the line, but Marchant proved awkward and resisted the takeover. He would not hand over the works to anyone, he said, and set his navvies to guard the plant and works. The company's men were turned away by the navvies when they appeared to take over the construction work at the tunnel, bitter arguments and scuffles occurred, and as a result things rapidly approached a stalemate position.

Exasperated, Brunel decided to take a hand in the matter. He summoned his assistant Varden and they went to the tunnel accompanied by a score of men to effect the takeover. However, Marchant had got wind of this action, and complained to the local Magistrate, telling him to come to the tunnel and read the Riot Act as things could become rather nasty if not contained.

When Brunel's party arrived they found themselves faced with the Magistrates, who told them to back off or things might get out of hand and a breach of the peace could be committed. Brunel duly retired to his hotel to consider what to do next. He and his men went back to the tunnel the following morning, but the Magistrates were still there, accompanied by a band of policemen armed with cutlasses. Brunel was on one side and Marchant and his navvies on the other, and tempers were rising.

The navvies eyed one another, itching for a fight. One of the Magistrates read out the Riot Act twice, then withdrew – the navvies had been warned! By now Varden and Brunel were acting like generals, and were considering anything that might wrest the control of the works and plant from Marchant. But they did not want to get into a fracas with the police, so they tried to make the Magistrates think that they had gone home, worn out after their unsuccessful attempts to get control over the construction of the tunnel. However, they planned to return and surprise Marchant and regain the initiative.

Brunel called up reinforcements and the navvies marched through the night from other parts of the railway. Villages were awakened by the men marching through the darkness – luckily they did no any damage en route – and a force of some 2,000 men subsequently amassed under Brunel's control. He was showing Marchant his strength, but still Marchant refused to hand over, so at around 2 am on the Monday morning the battle commenced.

Some 200 men went to the Worcester end of the tunnel, where Marchant met them and threatened them; they backed off, but with shovels and pick-axe shafts ready for action. Then Brunel ordered his men to attack. The navvies pushed Marchant out of the way and hit one of the enemy on the head with a shovel; he had pulled out a pistol although had not attempted to use it. He was not badly hurt, and several other minor injuries were inflicted on both sides.

Marchant retired to consider the position. He decided to get the police back, and a short time later some 30 policemen and soldiers from the Gloucester Artillery and two Magistrates appeared. Meanwhile some fighting was in progress and limbs were broken, but Brunel had men in reserve as another 200 had arrived from Warwick. The protagonists stood facing one another again, then one of the Magistrates suggested that Marchant should set his men back to work. However, Peto & Betts's men tried to stop them, and fighting broke out again – mere skirmishes, but fighting nonetheless. One man had his little finger bitten off and another had his head broken. Finally, after discussion with his advisers, Marchant decided that as he was outnumbered he would give way. He and Brunel met and agreed to let the whole matter go to arbitration.

Many other stories are known about the antics of the navvies, but it is acknowledged that when they did work, they worked very well and used their muscle to good use. Looking at the railways of Great Britain one can easily forget that the majority of the lines were laid by these same navvies using the most primitive of equipment and methods. Although vilified for their rumbustious behaviour, we should not forget that their sheer strength produced miracles as well as mayhem.

17
Violence at Mark Beech

*A*lthough large-scale railway construction in the British Isles had begun in the 1830s, by the 1860s West Kent and East Sussex were still poorly served by railways. This area, bordered by the Thames estuary in the north, the English Channel in the south and east and an imaginary line from London to Brighton in the west, was mainly agricultural in nature and there was little industry. Populations in those days were large enough, but the railway companies envisaged the growth of industry and housing, and realised the need to provide passenger and freight facilities.

The London, Chatham & Dover Railway controlled most of the tracks along the Thames estuary to the Medway towns and Canterbury, and had submitted a plan for an extension to Dover with further plans to reach Swanley and Sevenoaks, thence from Faversham to Margate, and these ambitions were fulfilled. However, the activities of the rival London, Brighton & South Coast Railway were being noted. The LB&SCR was a very ambitious company and its idea was to extend its grip on many areas of the railway system, and it would fight off any other company that showed any interest in routes that it had planned for itself. It even formed a 'front' company, the Surrey & Sussex Junction Railway Company, which was an independent company but sufficient to head off possible competition in those areas.

The LB&SCR had formulated plans to build a railway from Croydon through the North Downs to Oxted, then on to Edenbridge and through the High Weald of Kent to Groombridge. This route would provide a direct line from London via Tunbridge Wells to Eastbourne and Newhaven. The two companies shared the cost and appointed Messrs Waring Brothers of London as contractors. The Waring brothers, William, Henry and Charles, were aggressive in their business methods, and Charles became an MP in 1865.

Unfortunately many problems arose with the construction and the work began to cost much more than first anticipated; what is more, it began to fall behind schedule. But the main reason for things going wrong was the work of digging the three-quarter-mile-long tunnel through the 450-foot escarpment of the High Weald south of Edenbridge.

The tunnel passed more or less under the hamlet of Mark Beech and beneath the estate of the Talbot family at Falconhurst. Its northern portal was to be near the site of a station at Cowden, and a new station was planned at Edenbridge; the line was then to cross the River Eden just east of Edenbridge Mill, then meander along to Hever, where a new station was to be built.

It is said that around 700 to 1,000 men were used on the construction of Mark Beech tunnel, and of course, as in many major construction works at that time, labourers and navvies of all nationalities would be used. These itinerant labourers often caused great problems wherever they went – they had no regard for the local population, they stole, they poached, they had no fear of the police, they drank to excess, they lived in very rough conditions and usually had their children and camp followers hanging on. More important, they caused serious problems with public health. They were feared and despised, but they could work long hours for a pittance and they thus suited the railway contractors, who were just as perverse.

Any railway was difficult to construct and the hacking out of Mark Beech tunnel was to be no exception. The different nationalities thrown together in this case sparked off each other; although most of the workers were English, Warings took on some French-speaking engineers and overseers, added to which from time to time Belgian and French navvies appeared. Differentials in pay did not help the smouldering animosity evident on the site. Warings were as much to blame for the unrest. They wanted the most work for the least pay, and they got the kind of workforce they paid for. What started out as petty thieving grew to minor cases of violence, and with the heavy drinking the atmosphere was soon that of unbridled hostility.

Superintendent Richard Dance of Tonbridge spent a day at Mark Beech and was very disturbed at the situation that was developing. He heard some of the talk in the two pubs, the Victoria Arms and the Kentish Horse, and had the clear impression that trouble was just around the corner. He returned to Tonbridge and arranged for a number of his men to meet him at Mark Beech on the following Monday morning.

However, at approximately 8.30 on the Sunday night the hatred that had been festering for so long erupted when some of the English navvies started breaking windows and smashing the rough huts in the encampment. Foreign navvies, who were thought by the English to be after their jobs, were set upon and beaten up, and the fighting and violence was still rife an hour later. Dance's fears had been proved right and a real problem was now developing.

Then at about 11.30 pm some 50 men led by John Clarke and James Smith stormed Brooke House, a lodging house that took in the navvies. The attackers called that they wanted all foreigners out of the house. When the landlord, John West, would not comply, the gang broke into the house and started vandalising the interior; meanwhile, most of the foreigners had escaped through another door. John West had also escaped and managed to get to Cowden where he found the two local policemen, William Solly and George Bassett.

Luckily William Stanbrook, who worked for Warings as Inspector of Masonry, was lodging nearby and he accompanied the others to Mark Beech tunnel to see what was going on. When they got near the works they saw that they could do no good as they would be caught up with the fighting men. Bassett was therefore sent to Tonbridge for reinforcements. By 5 am Bassett, Superintendent Dance and 12 constables arrived at the tunnel. Dance decided to ask for more yet support and told the Chief Constable at Maidstone, Commander Ruxton, of the severity of the situation.

Meanwhile the French navvies had taken fright and had fled down the line to Edenbridge fearing for their lives. When Dance returned to Mark Beech he found a state of devastation. Most of the huts had been smashed beyond repair and at the tunnel mouth about 200 English navvies stood guarding the entrance. Armed with shovels, pick-axe handles and an assortment of weapons, they goaded the police, calling out 'Come and get us!' as they retreated into the tunnel.

Dance was aghast at the rapidly deteriorating situation, but soon he was joined by the Chief Constable who told him that 100 infantrymen were available at Shorncliffe Barracks, Folkestone, and could be moved to Mark Beech if necessary. By now about 100 policemen commanded by the Chief Constable and two Superintendents were at the scene, and it looked as if battle might commence at any time. Most local shopkeepers had taken the precaution of boarding up their premises as they feared that the hostilities might overspill into their area. The residents in the locality also locked themselves into their homes to escape the potential calamity.

The Chief Constable arranged his men between the two sides hoping to keep them apart if one side should decide to hurl themselves upon their enemies. Happily, the sight of the strong police presence seemed to have a calming effect on the protagonists, and the expected battle did not take place, although isolated fighting broke out in the town. As the foreigners tried to find sanctuary in the locked properties, the English navvies set upon them and beat them up, but the rumours that abounded of death and destruction proved to be untrue.

The heat now seemed to go out of the situation with the show of police force and the realisation that law and order would prevail; the prospect of jail was beckoning to the criminal elements. Most of the French labourers were transferred to other railway sites near Oxford, and the affair drew to its close when two Justices of the Peace enroled a few local people as Special Constables. These public-minded folk were to support the police and go to Mark Beech to arrest the English ringleaders; the police had decided to act before further trouble erupted.

As luck would have it confrontation was avoided, possibly because the presence of the officers had an effect on the hot-heads who sought a fight. However, further trouble was expected and the police decided to arrest three men who had been instrumental in fermenting the unrest. Shortly afterwards, seven more men were arrested, and they appeared in court at Tonbridge charged with numerous offences including riotous assembly, malicious damage, threatening behaviour and theft. In October the ten men appeared at West Kent Quarter Sessions at Maidstone; three of them were acquitted of the charges, but seven were sentenced to jail for a year with hard labour.

It is easy to blame the navvies for the many instances of trouble such as this that they instigated during the construction of the railways of Great Britain. They were certainly people that you didn't argue with, but their work rate when sober was phenomenal. Despite their drinking and sometimes violent behaviour, one must appreciate the terrible conditions in all weathers with which they had to contend, and consider the feats of engineering that they achieved, hacking tunnels out of solid rock, building bridges and aqueducts across broad valleys, tackling and draining bogs and many other major projects. And all this for a mere pittance because the construction companies either could not afford to, or simply *would not*, pay better wages.

18
The fatal error

Moving on a century or more, we arrive at a sinister tale of injury and death to the public at the hands of a railway employee. On a March night in the 1960s the overnight mail express to Edinburgh, consisting of 11 coaches and hauled by 'Deltic' locomotive No 9004 *Queen's Own Highlander*, was speeding to the northern terminal at 75 mph when the rear five coaches left the track and ploughed into the ballast, overturning and killing five passengers. One might wonder what it was on that level, straight length of track that caused this catastrophe. Certainly the powers that be in British Railways were very puzzled, and the most stringent investigations were conducted to ascertain the cause of the accident.

The crash happened just before midnight at Conington South signal box south of Peterborough, and fire crews from all over the area hastened to the scene. Several hundred yards of track had been ripped up by the derailed coaches which, leaving the track, had dug deep into the ballast and track formation. The coaches had to be jacked up to release the injured, and as dawn lit the wintry sky, the sight of the vehicles lying on their sides in the deep furrows of ballast, and the debris of people's possessions – books, clothes and burst-open suitcases scattered over the area – made a grim picture.

After the dead and injured passengers had been taken to hospital, over 150 men moved in swiftly to clear the wreckage and re-lay the track. The 'Deltic' and the five coaches that had stayed on the track were taken on to Peterborough for examination to try to find if clues to the cause of the incident could be found.

British Railways set up a high-level inquiry and tests were set up to examine the stress levels of the 'Buckeye' safety couplings used between the engine and coaches of the train, as one of them had been broken. However, the tests revealed that the break had happened *after* the derailment. These couplings were regularly examined as a matter of routine before a train set off on a journey. In addition, this particular stretch of track was regularly examined for ballast packing, and as the line was, and still is, subject to high-speed running, its condition was maintained to high standards.

However, on close examination it was found that the point switch blade was 'bruised', and wedged under the point was a piece of cast iron, but it could not have been there before the derailment. The Permanent Way Inspector from Peterborough couldn't understand why there were no marks made by the wheels going over the rail, and he did not accept that the derailment had been caused by some object having been placed over or under the rail, thus causing the wheels to leave the track.

So the mystery deepened; no conclusive evidence could be found for the derailment. Tests on one of the derailed coaches' bodies failed to reveal any fault. At the subsequent Ministry of Transport inquiry held at Liverpool Street station and presided over by Lt Col I. K. McNaughton, the signalman at Conington South, who had seen the crash, gave his evidence.

He said that he first saw the express when it was about three-quarters of a mile away. When it passed his box he saw the fourth coach from the end 'rear up'. He heard cracking and banging and saw the ballast being torn up and flying in all directions. This spectacle lasted for about half a minute.

Then the signalman mentioned a spell of one and a half seconds when he replaced his Home signal to its 'on', or Danger, position. He did this after the train had passed, and he avowed that he most definitely did not replace it until he saw the end of the express go by. Thus British Railways was so far unable to find a cause for the crash, and clearly further investigations had to be made.

Nevertheless, the acting Divisional Movement Manager at King's Cross sent the Conington man a memo 12 days after the crash, charging him with three irregularities as a result of exhaustive enquiries into the possibilities of a signalling error or a lack of concentration by the signalman. The charges were that he replaced the signal to Danger before the last coach had cleared the junction point, that he sent the 'Train out Section' signal before the train had covered a quarter of a mile beyond the main signal, and that he failed to send an 'Obstruction Danger' signal to the Abbots Ripton and Conington North signal boxes immediately after he became aware of the crash.

In reply, the signalman admitted the charge that he had contravened the regulations, and had no defence for the first two charges. To the third one he said, 'My only defence is that I was shocked and the sheer magnitude of the mishap caused my reactions to be temporarily slowed down.'

Then more than a year after the crash a warrant was issued for the signalman's arrest in connection with the Conington rail disaster. He was formally charged with the manslaughter of the five rail crash victims and with endangering the lives of railway passengers.

It was revealed that he had been previously discharged from the services suffering from 'hysteria and immature personality', but when he applied for a job as a signalman with British Railways no request was made to his former employer for any details of his health, either mental or physical. Lt Col McNaughton's inquiry revealed this glaring omission; apparently only his physical fitness was checked when he applied for the job, and the facts of his mental problems were not known to the BR management at the time of his application.

The signalman, by then no longer with BR, appeared at Nottingham Assizes. After two days of legal argument, the judge ruled that the jury should hear evidence regarding statements that the accused had made in the summer following the accident, to a signalman on duty at Abbots Ripton signal box. The latter said that the accused had told him that he would make some money out of the story of the rail crash. He went on to say that he intended to approach a national newspaper and tell them how he wrecked the 'Flying Scotsman'!

Two sets of bogie wheels were on display at the Court House in Nottingham for examination by the jury at the trial. I don't suppose they learned very much about the performance of the wheels under the adverse circumstances that caused the crash. However, evidence was revealed at the trial that a plunger which locked the points in the track where the five coaches were derailed had been removed within 24 hours of the occurrence, and not 50 hours as shown in the signal box records. According to the record book, which showed every movement in the working shift, the points lock plunger had an oil slick that proved it had been moved within 24 hours of the examination – which would have been just after the crash.

The former signalman stated that he had replaced the Home signal as soon as the train had passed it, instead of waiting until the train had passed over the points. He had then accidentally unlocked the points by pulling another lever, No 26. Realising his mistake he had made a grab for it and moved the next one, No 27, which had opened the points. In effect he had opened the points under the fifth coach, which caused the wheels to split the blade and ride over on to the ballast, thus dragging the other four coaches with them. No wonder he saw the end coach rear up.

The noise of the crash was heard by the signalman at Conington

North, and he immediately telephoned the South box to enquire what
had happened. The signalman there replied that 'the signals are in
order and the train appears to have stopped'. The train had stopped all
right, but the back five coaches were on their sides in the ballast and
five passengers had died. The Conington South man appeared to be
very calm at the time according to fellow signalmen who spoke to him.
It was as if he didn't realise the enormity of the events that had taken
place.

The accused stated in reply to the police, 'I tried to get myself to
believe that I was not to blame . . . the thought of the death of those
five people has been with me since that night. Despite my uncalculated
action I did not at any time intend to cause the deaths of those people,
the wrecking of the train or any other damage.'

When the police suggested that it could not have happened
accidentally, the other replied, 'You know damned well it didn't. I knew
what I was doing, but I didn't intend to derail the train. It was a sort of
force of habit.'

The court was told that the signalman had been a junior musician in
the services but, as already stated, he was discharged because he suffered
from 'hysteria and immature personality'. After leaving British
Railways employment after the accident he returned to the services as
a musician, and was described as a 'brilliant' and very artistically gifted
musician.

As regards other aspects of the case, Rule 68a(i) of the British
Railways Rule Book states that 'at a junction, the signal immediately in
rear of and protecting such junction must be placed at Danger as soon
as the last vehicle has cleared the junction points'. Clearly the
signalman hadn't obeyed the rule. It was quite obvious from the official
inquiry that the points had not been open to direct traffic from the
down line to the down goods line before the engine reached the points.
The engine and the first six coaches had passed safety over the points
and were not damaged in any way. But as the seventh coach was
actually passing over the points they were opened or partially opened,
and the wheels at the rear of the seventh coach passed between the
switch rail and the stop rail, causing the disaster.

The prosecution accepted the accused's plea of not guilty to five
charges of manslaughter, but he pleaded guilty to the charge of
endangering the safety of passengers by the unlawful operation of
signals and points in Conington South signal box.

After due consideration, the jury returned a formal verdict of guilty.
The judge, as he passed a sentence of two years imprisonment, spoke of
the signalman's bad habits, which as he knew were breaches of the rules
that were designed for the purpose of safeguarding passengers.

In retrospect the verdict was rather strange. The signalman's unreliable ways and scant respect for the basic rules in the directing of high-speed traffic had killed five people, on a section of track that warranted the most circumspect and totally reliable personnel to operate the railway system.

It is ironic that this section of railway track had been the scene of other tragedies. In December 1961 a terrible crash occurred when four goods trains collided, blocking both sets of tracks. One of the goods trains had become derailed and the other trains on adjacent lines had run into the wreckage. Luckily only three people were injured.

Then in September 1966 a light engine collided with the rear of a King's Cross night express. Again injuries were light, with five people being taken to hospital for treatment for shock, bruises and abrasions.

And way back in October 1948 a well-known and respected citizen of Peterborough, Col A. H. Mellows, had been killed in his car when the vehicle was hit by a train as he was driving across the level crossing. In March of the same year six German prisoners of war had been killed on the same crossing when their 3-ton lorry had been hit by a train.

Apparently Col Mellows and his large black Chrysler car make occasional appearances to this day, in spirit form, perhaps as a reminder of those unfortunate incidents that cost so many lives.

19
'This man has to be caught'

A more conventional but nonetheless horrific example of violence on the railway occurred on a May day some years ago, when a 19-year-old French girl was the victim of a savage attack on board a train that rendered her unconscious. She had noticed her assailant peering into her compartment on the London-bound suburban train as it waited to proceed, then he had got into the compartment. She was completely unprepared for was the sudden attack that followed, as he threw himself upon her; his assault left her quite unable to defend herself, but after the pent-up fury of his molestation subsided, to her surprise he began to apologise and talk quite rationally. She told him that he ought to see a doctor, to which he replied that he had already done so!

As the train drew into the terminus he leapt out before it had stopped and vanished into the crowds of people doing their battle with London's rush hour. The girl reported the incident to the police and was examined by a doctor who treated her for shock. She was able to give a good account of the attack and co-operated fully with the railway police; after a while she was taken home and the police started their enquiries into this latest in a far too frequent series of attacks upon women.

A photographer took several pictures of the marks on the girl's neck, which showed that attempts had been made to strangle her. The case was frightening, and the police feared that the man might strike again, with perhaps fatal results. The girl had impressed the police with her calmness and detail; she spoke very good English and thought that she might recognise her assailant again. The remark that he had made to her about having seen a doctor gave the distinct impression that he might have been undergoing treatment for a mental problem, and enquiries were made in all the local hospitals in the area.

A 'photofit' picture assembled by the police from the girl's description was circulated throughout the area in the hope that somebody would recognise the man. Naturally medical staff are very protective towards their patients to avoid them being further upset by police enquiries, so a 'softly softly' approach was taken. However, one Nursing Officer made the suggestion that the man might have been a former patient of a doctor who now lived in the West Country, and the local police were asked to look into the matter.

Meanwhile other possibilities were being examined and other suspects interviewed, and the search for information did bring forth some useful details. The crew of the train and another railway employee did remember seeing a man fitting the 'photofit' description walking along the platform at the station where the assailant boarded the train, looking into the compartments as if looking for someone in particular. They then saw him jump aboard the train just as it moved off. The police decided to try a blanket coverage of every station along the route taken by the girl; the 'photofit' picture was prominently displayed and anyone who recognised the wanted man was asked to speak to one of the many police officers in the area, then a questionnaire would be filled in. A team of police officers travelled on the trains and showed each passenger the picture; passengers were also asked to complete the questionnaire.

The public was, as always, very co-operative, and some of the pieces of the jigsaw began to be slotted into place. The police also got the message on the television programme *Police File*, so the coverage stood a fair chance of success. However, the police were not to know what a cunning character they were dealing with at this stage in the investigation.

The particular suspect already mentioned to the police turned out to be employed in a London office. When questioned about the offence he insisted that he had been at work that afternoon, and a young lady in the same office verified his statement. He had, however, gone off sick the day after the incident, and was known to have convicted for indecent exposure, mostly on trains. The police therefore checked his alibi with the utmost thoroughness.

The usual routine enquiries continued, and at least five other suspects had to be found, interviewed and perhaps eliminated from the case. The police felt that time was at a premium, as they considered that the assailant might strike again with more serious consequences. Their efforts brought forth another possible suspect: a man who answered the description of the wanted man was observed travelling to and from the station where the assailant had boarded the train. When the police questioned him it appeared that he was 'chatting up' a pretty young Swiss girl. He also had convictions for indecency and admitted that he had been on the station on the afternoon in question; however, he strongly denied that he had attacked the French girl and volunteered to take part in an identification parade – but nobody picked him out.

The police therefore concentrated on the other suspect's alibi, that he had been in his office on the day of the attack. The young lady who had supported his alibi now said that she could have been mistaken, and that he had been in the office all the *previous* day. The police now spoke to *all* the staff in the office, and it transpired that he had *not* been in the office at the time of the attack. So where was he? The police considered that he had had time to leave the office, travel to out of London and commit the offence.

As was his wont, the man admitted himself into a mental hospital as a voluntary patient, a favourite trick when the police got too close. Three police officers interviewed him at the hospital, but he was very evasive and, in fact, questioned them! The police were very cautious in what they told him, and he still maintained that he was at work and was totally innocent of the alleged attack. He told the police that he had had a date with a young girl at 6 pm on the day of the attack; he was now desperately trying to confuse them with his alibis in an attempt to throw them off the scent. The police did, however, manage to persuade him to take part in an identification parade.

The girl recognised him immediately, then broke down; she had been brave and calm but the trauma of the horrific event had caught up with her. The man still maintained his innocence and repeated that he was in his office at the time of the incident. He said that he was a married man who had parted from his wife, but his tales varied wildly and involved telephone calls to his wife, her parents and his doctor. His version, if true, made it quite impossible for him to have carried out the assault on the French girl.

The police, however, were not to be moved by his plausibility; they found clothing in his flat which the girl recognised, and other details were confirmed by other items they found there. It would appear that the police now had enough evidence to charge the man – with attempted murder. He still strenuously denied the charge, but the police had every reason to be satisfied with their efforts to bring him to account. They knew that they were dealing with a cunning, devious man who could be very plausible and knew all the tricks of the trade; his ability to use every available loophole to his advantage made him very difficult to pin down, and it was therefore imperative that any case against him must be completely bomb-proof!

As the Police investigation continued it became clear that they would have to dispel completely the alibis that their suspect had so carefully constructed to thwart their progress; this was to be a very painstaking process that would take time and diligent effort. Then an amazing fact emerged that added considerably to the case against the man – the day before the French girl was assaulted, the local police had received a report from a woman who said that she had been attacked by a man on as train in the same area; the Detective Sergeant who had seen her had said that she seemed highly strung and nervous, and he had formed the opinion that she had imagined it. Unfortunately the railway police had not been notified, and when they interviewed this lady she was able to impart considerable information that strengthened the case against the suspect. However, when an identification parade was arranged the lady was unable to pick out her assailant from the line-up.

The trial took place at the Central Criminal Court and the accused was charged with various charges of indecent assault, but the Director of Public Prosecutions decided that there was insufficient evidence to proceed with the attempted murder charge. The Defence reaffirmed the man's alibi, the accused still maintaining that he was at his place of work at the time of the attack. His various alibis consisted of various incidents that took place so closely together that it was difficult to unravel truth from invention; for example, he claimed that someone had been late for an appointment at his office that afternoon, proving he was there, but enquiries revealed that this person was *always* late for appointments; the accused had used that knowledge in another attempt to throw off any suspicion. Other red herrings were thrown about by the Defence, and all were disproved, but only after much hard work and diligence by the railway police.

But despite the best efforts of the Defence, the jury found the accused guilty on two charges of indecent assault. The court was told that he had ten previous convictions involving indecency on trains, but the Judge said that none of his previous convictions had involved an attack. The Judge sentenced him to four years imprisonment. When he was examined by doctors at the remand prison they decided that he was not insane according to the McNaughton Rules, and the examining doctor also emphasised that the prisoner was very adept at feigning certain mental illnesses, and had used this ploy to gain refuge in mental hospitals when the police attention became too close. Many people who were in close contact with him felt that he would kill one day if he was allowed his freedom; however, they felt that he should remain under treatment until some assessment could assure the authorities that he was no longer a danger.

20
The bridge

*I*t is a regrettable fact that bridges over railway lines have often been the location of suicides, where some poor soul has felt constrained to leap off in front of an approaching train. This somewhat bizarre case involved a station footbridge, and the intending suicide was a young lady in a state of anguished depression.

When she arrived at the station she walked on to the platform and slowly climbed the steps of the footbridge. Approaching the middle she gazed down on the scene beneath her – people milling around on the platforms, going about their daily routine, trains arriving and departing – then she climbed on to the parapet and sat there, her legs dangling over the edge.

By now the people on the platforms waiting for their trains were beginning to take notice of her precarious position on the bridge girders. A man pointed out her position to a porter, and they both naturally looked worried. The porter moved towards the steps leading to the bridge with an anxious look on his face. The girl saw him approach and called out, 'I'm going to kill myself, I'm going to jump off in front of a train, I'm going to kill myself!'

The porter, now most concerned, tried to get closer to her, but she was in a bad state and put her hand up to stop him coming any nearer. She was still on the parapet and he realised that one false move could result in her falling some 20 feet on to the track. The situation was in danger of developing into a dreadful tragedy, and the police were called. They tried to entice the girl off the parapet to safety – cups of tea were offered, but to no avail. The young lady was very distraught and still liable to jump.

Meanwhile all traffic on the railway had stopped, and a train waiting to set off was held. The passengers were puzzled by the delay, so left their train and went to see what was going on. Passing road traffic in the adjacent street was also taking an interest, motorists craning their necks to see the drama being enacted in the station. Even the local radio station arrived – what good they could do was questionable, but it was news.

The girl seemed determined to carry out her threat, or so she said, and the efforts of the police had so far been in vain. By now some of the passengers on the waiting train were getting very impatient, one man in particular, an ex-paratrooper. He was getting fed up with the ineffectual efforts of the police and railway staff to get the girl off the bridge, and after some 40 minutes' delay his annoyance was increasing. From his vantage point he thought that the person on the bridge was a young man, and flinging down his suitcase he headed for the bridge. A policeman told him to get off, but he went storming up the steps and walked towards the girl. Pushing his way through the people gathered there, he shouted, 'Either jump or get down!', then the horrified crowd of onlookers saw him push her off the parapet 20 feet on to the railway tracks below.

Remarkably she survived, although she sustained multiple injuries, and the passenger was arrested. A man of previously exemplary character, in court he admitted inflicting grievous bodily harm on his victim, and as an ex-paratrooper said that he had been jumping out of planes all his life, and thought it was a man that was threatening to jump. 'I thought the bloke would land on his feet and leg it. I thought I was doing the right thing. If I had known it was a woman, I wouldn't have done it.'

Jailing the man for 15 months, the Judge remarked, 'I am satisfied that you acted in a fit of uncharacteristic temper'. As for the girl, she was admitted to hospital for a very long stay, and a lengthy period of treatment to help her overcome her terrible experience.

21
The bombers

I remember reading some years ago about the legendary exploits of Lawrence of Arabia and his battles with the Turks in Mesopotamia during the years 1917-18. Lawrence with his gallant men was trying to stop the Turks and their allies from over- running this part of the world, but today he would be described as a terrorist who used every means devised by man to stop an implacable enemy. One of Lawrence's ploys was to attack the railway by which the Turks transported men and equipment; sections of the line would be blown up in strategic places where the most destruction and inconvenience could be caused. Points were and are the most vulnerable parts of a railway track, taking up a lot of time and effort to replace.

Today we associate such acts with terrorist organisations like the IRA, and think of them as a modern phenomenon, but an early terrorist act by Irish nationalists occurred in February 1884 when an explosion ripped through a cloakroom at London's Victoria station, causing considerable damage and injuring two people who were waiting for their train. The following day a search was made of all the cloakrooms of all the stations in London, and three further explosive devices were found similar to the one that had exploded at Victoria. These were described by the press as 'infernal machines', and consisted of a clock and several pounds of dynamite connected to a pistol loaded and cocked to fire when the hands of the clock reached a certain time. They were very unreliable and the three found elsewhere in other London stations had failed to detonate and were rendered safe. It was stated by the press that these bombs were the work of the 'Fenian Brotherhood'.

In 1939 an IRA bombing campaign targeted trains, stations and other railway properties where the maximum disruption could be caused. This time acid bombs were used, and as a result of their work at several stations one man died and others were injured. As this series of outrages proceeded it was obvious that cloakrooms and left luggage repositories were very vulnerable, and it was decided that no packages would be accepted in cloakrooms unless they had first been inspected by the railway police. These measures seemed to work and the IRA gave up its efforts, at least for the time being.

These events also had a marked effect on the activities of the safe-breaking fraternity, who had been using gelignite to blow open safes. They did not want to be stopped and questioned about the packages they might be carrying, as they might be suspected of belonging to the IRA and conviction would result in a very long prison sentence. Some cloakroom attendants got quite twitchy over any ticking noise, but it was usually found to be the office clock!

However, at 8.48 am on Thursday 4 March 1976 a terrible explosion wrecked the roof and interior of a ten-coach set as it left Cannon Street for the sidings. Luckily the train was empty, but at the time a Cannon Street to Gravesend train was passing; the windows of the leading coach were smashed and the side pitted with fragments of the blast. Eight people were injured, mainly by flying glass, and were treated in hospital, although they were all discharged about an hour later. All emergency services were called out and the hunt for the perpetrators was begun. Loud-speaker messages were broadcast at every station asking for anyone with any information about any person seen to be acting suspiciously to come forward to assist the police. The police also asked the public to fill in questionnaires as regards seating plans in trains. Every effort was used to seek information, and the public co-operated magnificently.

It was very obvious that the perpetrators of this unsuccessful outrage had been determined to inflict as much injury and disruption on the public as possible; a bomb of that kind exploding on a crowded train would have been catastrophic, but luckily fate decreed otherwise.

The outrage at Cannon street sparked off more attacks on London's transport system. At 4.50 pm on Monday 15 March an explosion occurred in the leading coach of a train that had just left West Ham station; it is almost certain that a terrorist had the device with him, intending to leave it on the train when he got off further down the line. It is also thought that the terrorist had been adjusting the timing mechanism and the electric fuse had begun to speed up. He had thrown the device away from him, it had exploded and he was injured. Very fortunately the train was lightly loaded as it was not the rush hour, but eight passengers still received slight injuries. The terrorist then tried to get off the train, which had stopped; he made for the motorman's cab and scrambled out on to the track, blood streaming from his face. The motorman chased him along the track, but the man turned to see his pursuer, dragged out a gun and shot him dead at point blank range. Another passenger, a 18-year-old Post Office worker, nearly caught him, but he again used his gun to shoot and seriously wound his pursuer. A policeman arrived to help and came face to face with the killer – two more shots were fired as the bomber tried to find cover. Two more policemen chased the man along the track and cornered him; he then turned the gun on himself, and was taken to hospital in a serious condition. None of the policemen were armed, and they behaved in a very brave manner to tackle such a dangerous criminal. It was thought that the same man might have been responsible for the earlier explosion near Cannon Street.

The emergency was not over yet because the very next day the terrorists struck again. An explosion on a Piccadilly line train ripped through a carriage, which burst open slightly injuring a passenger who was waiting on the platform. Again good fortune played a part – the train had emptied its passengers, or terrible loss of life would have occurred. Just after 2 am the next morning a 5 lb device was found in an empty train at Neasden carriage sidings. The woman cleaner who found it had a very lucky escape from injury – she picked it up and threw it out on to the ground, and it was later defused by the police explosives department. The most dangerous aspect of any bombing campaign is the fact that some of the devices do not go off and have to be made safe later, which is always a very hazardous occupation.

One can say much about the public's phlegmatic approach to these terrorist campaigns against the community; people refused to be frightened from going to and from their work and leisure activities, and life went on much as before. As the result of police investigations, three 'bomb factories' were discovered and a number of people arrested in connection with the outrages. It is a sobering to consider what might have happened with dedicated terrorists like the IRA.

As well as highly populated main-line stations, the railways of this country include many miles of remote track, isolated signal boxes and sidings, and the railway police have used constant vigilance and a high state of awareness to foil any attempts of further terrorist attacks. However, the covert terrorist is difficult to catch and his deadly work only takes seconds.

The police have asked the general public to 'Be your own security officer and watch out for unattended packages'. What more can be done?

Part Four: Murder

22
'In the execution of his duty'

*W*hen robbery and violence come together, it often leads inevitably to murder, and, as we have already seen, it is the officers of the railway police who bear the brunt of violent lawlessness.

Railway wagons sitting in sidings are always vulnerable to theft; however securely locked there are thieves who will attempt to get in and remove the contents. The railway police have had the unenviable job of keeping vigilance on remote sidings to deter the thieves whose ingenuity seemingly knows no bounds, and they have had many successes in bringing to justice those responsible for looting railway vehicles. Inevitably, however, some of the rogues are so clever that the surveillance has to be that bit more prolonged to achieve a successful conclusion.

To the man in the street the prevention of crime on the railway system is the same as that on the street, and in many respects it is similar, but the railway police are a minority force and do not have the numbers to match their civil counterparts. They therefore need to rely on the civil forces to assist them in the pursuance of law and order.

Over the years many police officers have been injured in the course of their work,and some have unfortunately met a premature death serving the cause of justice. One such was Detective Sergeant Robert Kidd, who joined the LNWR police as a constable in 1885. In 1887 he found himself at Warrington as a Detective, and after a year was posted to Edgehill. The following year he was transferred to Manchester, and was made up to Detective Sergeant. At 37 years old he was regarded very highly as a capable, thorough and likeable officer.

One autumn some goods wagons that were located in the goods yard at Wigan were being pilfered from, and a local detective named Osbourne had kept a watch in the yard for about six weeks without any success in apprehending the miscreants. Osbourne was joined by Det

Sgt Kidd on Saturday 29 September and they met in the subway of the passenger station. Osbourne handed Kidd a cap to wear instead of his uniform hat – it looked less conspicuous – and they set off for the sidings. There was a bright moon and visibility was good. When they reached a certain spot Osbourne halted and looked around the corner of a wall. He had spotted a man who was later identified as William Halliwell.

Halliwell was on his knees, but when Osbourne spoke to him, on seeing the two policemen, he ran off. Osbourne gave chase and knocked the other man to the ground, then dragged him to his feet and pinned him up against a wagon. Aided by Kidd, a furious struggle took place, but Osbourne had the measure of his suspect, then another man appeared and fell over Osbourne and his prisoner. This man was to be identified as William Kearsley, and Osbourne pulled out his truncheon just as yet another man appeared from behind a wagon. Osbourne saw that the man had something bright in his hand, and he lashed out with his truncheon and caught the man a heavy blow on his hand. Despite their best efforts the three got away, Halliwell snatching Osbourne's truncheon.

The two policemen had been struggling with the three men for about 10 minutes. Osbourne now turned his attention to his superior officer. He found Kidd between a wall and a wagon on his knees – blood was running down his face and he seemed in a bad way. Osbourne tried to lift him but Kidd cried out in pain, asking for a drink of water. Osbourne was exhausted and he only managed to carry Kidd a few yards when he collapsed and fell to the ground with Kidd. He did not remember much until he awoke in hospital, but it emerged that he had managed to find a signal box and the signalman and loco men had helped him and the local police had been called.

The railway police were also soon on the scene and the hunt for the robbers was on. The nearby area was searched and two bloodstained caps were discovered. They also searched the wagons in the siding, and found on wagon No 12315 the sheet had been torn and the contents of sweets had been tampered with. Two other wagons had also been tampered with, but nothing was found to be missing. Det Sgt Kidd had been found nearby in a very bad way, and when he was taken to the passenger station he was found to have died from his horrific injuries – nine stab wounds in his head, face and neck, several other bruises and abrasions, injuries to his right knee and arm, and the severing of part of his index finger. He had obviously been in a terrible struggle, and in the yard was found two large pools of blood. Kidd had sold his life very dearly.

However, from information swiftly gleaned from the public, the railway police were able to apprehend the three villains very quickly. William Kearsley, who was the first to be arrested, was in an identification parade at the hospital where Osbourne was receiving treatment, and the policeman recognised him immediately. Elijah Winstanley, a collier, had been caught at 11.55 pm on 1 October, then another coal-miner, William Halliwell, after being arrested willingly gave evidence about the other two men. All three were accused of wilfully killing Robert Kidd by stabbing him with a sharp weapon and also assaulting and inflicting grievous bodily harm on William Henry Osbourne.

The case was brought before Wigan Borough Police Court, and Mr Kershaw, representing the prosecution, had been instructed by the LNWR. While making his opening statement he was constantly interrupted by Winstanley, who had become hysterical in the Dock and was crying out 'Kill me, kill me, it's murder, I did it! I didn't want to kill him!'

The story of their intent to rob the wagons came out very clearly. Halliwell, it seemed, was a thoroughly notorious character and his statement was not totally believable. He said that he had met Winstanley and Kearsley in the New Inn at Lower Ince, and they had then moved to the Fox Tavern; after more drinks they left the Fox and climbed over the fence into the sidings. They had been trying to force their way into the covered wagons to do petty thieving, but had only had success with one wagon when they had been surprised by Kidd and Osbourne. After the struggle they had got away and had met back at the Fox for a rest.

Halliwell had told the others that he did not think the man he had stabbed would live. 'I stabbed him many times,' he had admitted. Halliwell had then left and had spent the night on a boat on the nearby canal.

During the trial, much damaging evidence was revealed about the three men in the dock. Kearsley's daughter said that she remembered her father saying to her mother that 'our Elijah has been stabbing a bobby in the face and neck with a knife' (Winstanley was Kearsley's half-brother). When the police surgeon examined the three men he found that Winstanley had bruises and scrapes that were about two or three days old and were consistent with Det Osbourne's injuries. Both caps found at the scene of the crime were bloodstained, and when a pair of handcuffs belonging to Kidd were found nearby, they too had marks of blood on them. This case attracted great interest, and Kearsley and Winstanley were committed to Liverpool Assizes, while Halliwell was to appear at the Assizes charged with unlawful wounding.

That November some workmen playing cards in a field near the

LNWR line at Wigan found a penknife very close to the scene of the Kidd murder; it was given to the local police who eventually identified it as belonging to Winstanley.

The waiting time did not actually do Halliwell much good; he became hysterical and was in a very bad way when the day of the Liverpool Assizes began. The Judge advised the jury not to place much faith in the veracity of Halliwell's evidence. But the jury had heard enough to convince them of the guilt of Winstanley and Kearsley. Strangely enough, although Halliwell was charged with unlawful wounding, he was discharged as there was insufficient evidence to convict him. Kearsley, who had played a major role in the killing and could be considered as an accomplice to the foul deed, also faced the death penalty, but was reprieved and his sentence commuted to penal servitude, leaving Winstanley to mount the gallows.

A contemporary report in the Liverpool press of the time shows that Halliwell, who was the principal witness for the Crown, was discussed 'with bitter and resentful animation'. The *Manchester Courier* reported: 'Melancholy and mean are the details of the tragedy. It is above all things satisfactory that the culprits have been apprehended and brought to Justice. Policemen and detectives as the representatives of law and order must be supported in carrying out their duties at all costs. Their lot is not a particularly happy one at any time but it would become intolerable if the breakers of the law could molest them with impunity.'

The *Liverpool Mercury* spoke in severe terms and said, 'Not one particle of sympathy can be extended to miscreants of this character who, to save the consequences of petty larceny, do not shrink from sacrificing human life', and the *Liverpool Echo* wound things up with its comment, 'There yet remains the appeal to the prerogative of mercy, but in the special circumstances of the case, the murdered man having been a Policeman in the execution of his duty, it would be unwise to hold out any hope of respite'.

There was indeed no hope for Winstanley. He paid the ultimate price for murder, and said as he mounted the gallows that he would rather die at the end of a rope than serve 20 years' penal servitude.

Many thieves have been arrested by railway police officers at Wigan in the century and more since Kidd died, and it is an unfortunate fact that sidings used for the storage of wagons containing valuable contents will always be the target for would-be thieves.

23
The murder of
Railway Detective Hibbs

*A*s we have just seen, the railway policemen's lot was never a happy one. They have always been stretched for numbers, and the job was often lonely and subject to attack from anyone disturbed while breaking the law. Another similar event a few years later was to cost a loyal London & North Western Railway detective his life while pursuing his job in keeping a watch on company property.

It was Saturday 10 August 1901, and Railway Detective Thomas Hibbs was patrolling the area around Curzon Street Goods Depot in Birmingham. In the depot yard were several coal wagons stacked with bags of coal waiting for the local coal merchants to collect them. Reports of bags of coal having been stolen had been received for the past few weeks and the railway company were keen to stop the practice. The police were attempting to detain the thieves, but so far they had been too smart and no one had been caught. So far. . .

Railway Detective Hibbs knew the area well, and although he was aware of the danger of apprehending the thieves, he hoped that a blast from his whistle might bring help quite quickly. However, that August night things went very wrong for Thomas Hibbs. He was walking near the Curzon Street Depot when he heard noises and voices, and arrived just in time to see three men dragging sacks of coal through the gates. He shouted at them and gave chase.

They ran into Fazeley Street near the canal and Hibbs followed them. There they turned to face him, and, realising that he was out-numbered, he drew his night-stick and prepared to defend himself. The three men surrounded him and one threw himself at Hibbs, grabbing the staff. Hibbs lashed out and tried to prevent them from attacking him, but one of the men hit him hard on the back of the head and rendered him unconscious. They then picked him up and threw him into the canal, where he died of drowning. To all intents and purposes they had committed murder.

Birmingham Police acted fast, throwing their net wide. Two young men, Frank Parslow of Barns Street and Charles Webb of Drury Lane, were arrested. Parslow gave his age as 21, although he was actually 24 years of age, and stated that he was an out of work coach painter. Webb admitted to 18 years old, but his mates said he was 21; he was a brass caster's labourer, but also out of work. Another man was also arrested in connection with the incident, one William Billingsley, a labourer living in a court off Moseley Street. Parslow and Webb knew each other but had fallen out some time ago, or so they made out.

Witnesses had seen both Webb and Parslow near the scene of the crime, and both men made statements to the police. However, one of the witnesses received a letter threatening all kinds of consequences if the witness spoke out or assisted the police in their enquiries; the letter had bloodstains smeared over it. Another witness came forward and told the police that he had seen two young men near the scene of the crime, and that they were using language that suggested that they would revenge themselves upon someone. One of the young men then said 'My name is Webb', a strange thing to say in public. However, the witness had not been able to identify this man. Other people were able to testify that they had seen a number of young fellows in the area at the time that Detective Hibbs was attacked and killed, and one of these men made some reference to 'the man in the cut', but most of the evidence was indirect and circumstantial.

At the subsequent Coroner's Court a verdict of 'wilful murder by persons unknown' was accepted. The London & North Western Railway Company offered a reward of £100 for information that would result in the prosecution of the person or persons responsible for this cruel deed.

However, the circumstances of the incident were considered not strong enough as yet to charge the three men in custody. They were suspected of knowledge of, or having actually committed, the crime, they were at the scene of the crime and made statements concerning each other in relation to the crime, but the police were still making exhaustive investigations to substantiate their enquiries. One of the men, Billingsley, had insisted that the three men did not wish to do Hibbs any harm, and he persisted that the whole affair had started out as 'a bit of fun'. Hardly fun when one of your mates strikes someone a terrible blow on the back of the head, then you pick up the unconscious body and throw it into the canal.

These men had been caught red-handed stealing bags of coal, they had taken advantage of the fact that Hibbs was on his own, they had seen him as a threat to their success, so they had taken matters into their own hands and silenced him for ever. Yet despite these facts and the witnesses who had come forward, the police apparently could not pin any charge on to any of the defendants, and all three protested their innocence.

But what had happened to the bags of coal that they had so openly stolen from LNWR property? A search was made at Parslow's house and a coal sack was found; no convincing explanation as to where it came from was given, Mrs Parslow claiming that she had been given the sack by a Mrs Nixon who had lived in the house before them. Bound together by a code of conduct as strong as that of any secret society, there was at that time a certain class of Birmingham citizen that never told anyone anything; they just bided their time, then meted out their revenge in their own way.

The Railway Police were determined to bring the murderers to book, and didn't believe in the claims of circumstantial evidence as claimed by the civil police. They looked at the case logically and arrived at the conclusion stated above; they could not understand why the Birmingham police had arrested these three men but failed to make the charge stick.

On Friday 6 September 1901 the trial took place at the Victoria Court of the three men charged with the murder of Railway Detective Thomas Hibbs. Following a plea of insubstantial evidence by the three men's solicitor, the Stipendiary Magistrate directed that the trio should be conditionally discharged as insufficient evidence was available to charge them with the murder.

This crime is therefore yet to be solved. Over the years many attempts were made to re-open the case, but after many enquiries and searches for leads, nothing was found. Perhaps the answer lies in the Mafia-like secretive attitude found in that area, people protecting each other in times of need. Or perhaps the friends of the three men imposed their own type of punishment on the suspects, because even from the most flimsy evidence put forward it seems very plain that they *did* murder Hibbs and were guilty to their dying days of this most foul crime.

24
The ladder gang

*T*he civil police are the heroes of this tale of robbery and murder. On 27 October 1885 four criminals, whose reputations had spread nearly the length and breadth of the land, met at Gretna Green railway station. They were Anthony Benjamin Rudge, John Martin, James Baker and William Baker (no relation). These fellows also used various aliases for their nefarious deeds, and were regarded as vicious and highly unpredictable. When the four met in Gretna they planned an audacious burglary in the home of Sir Frederick Graham, who lived at Netherby Hall, a few miles from Carlisle.

The gang had histories of crime. Rudge, described as a dog-trainer, was a well-known dog thief, had been in prison many times and was currently wanted for robbery at Brixton. Martin was wanted for the murder at Romford, Essex, of a police Inspector whom he had shot while escaping after a burglary. James Baker had a reputation as a receiver of stolen goods, and William Baker had also been in Her Majesty's prisons on numerous occasions for theft with violence. A bright lot indeed!

When they arrived at Gretna by a special train that had been hired by the Longtown Coursing Meeting, each carried a case, and these were left in the Station Master's office. They left the station and had a good look around the village and surrounding area; they also questioned several local people and learned that the Graham family was in residence. They dined at the Bush Hotel in Longtown that night and made their plans to burgle Netherby Hall the next day.

The following afternoon James Baker collected one of the cases from the station and re-joined the others in the Graham Arms inn, which was about 100 yards from the station at Gretna. But while they were drinking, some sharp-eyed local saw one of the men 'doing something with a key' – possibly making a wax impression. He told the landlord what he had seen, but the bar was busy and the incident was soon forgotten.

Later that day Baker returned to the railway station and asked the Station Master to forward the case to Carlisle for a 'Mr A. Smith, who would pick it up'. The October daylight had gone when the gang entered the spacious grounds of Netherby Hall. They gained access to the house silently and without detection. At 8 pm a housemaid found the door to Lady Hermione Graham's room locked on the inside, and told the butler, who managed to climb a ladder and gain entry. He discovered that a considerable amount of valuable jewellery was missing from a dressing case that had been broken open. Means of entry to the room had been effected by a ladder and good finger-marks were clearly shown on the window sill. However, in those days forensic science was in its infancy and the police had not the means to value the evidence so kindly left by the criminals.

After the discovery of the crime Sir Frederick Graham sent his grooms on horseback to tell the police at Kingstown and also to search the surrounding countryside for signs of the gang. Information was sent to Carlisle and all local roads were kept under observation. The gang were first seen near Kingstown later that evening by Sergeant Roche and PC Johnson of the local Constabulary; these officers challenged the men and the reply was two revolver shots. The gang made off, the police in pursuit, but the fugitives turned and fired more shots and the two officers were hit and wounded, one in the shoulder and the other in the thigh. The burglars ran down the embankment on to the railway line and disappeared in the direction of Carlisle.

Around 11 pm a policeman at Gosling Dyke stopped four strangers, but one of them pulled out a revolver and the solitary policeman had no alternative but to let them pass. The police were by now, according to the local press, acting with 'unusual energy', and the countryside for miles around had been roused by this dramatic turn of events.

At around 2 am on the morning of 29 October the signalman at Dalston Road Crossing on the North Eastern Railway in the western outskirts of Carlisle thought he heard noises outside the box, then he heard footsteps in the ballast and, looking out of the window, he saw three men on the line heading in the direction of Carlisle. When he opened the signal box door they heard him and scattered; luckily a policeman had gone to the signal box to warn the occupant of the dangerous gang and he was just in time to see them disappearing into the darkness. He gave chase and when the gang saw him they turned on him and beat him unconscious with sticks and the butts of their pistols.

The gang then left the railway line and headed back on to the road. The constable regained consciousness and staggered back to the signal box, but by this time the thieves were well away. Two of them were then reported in a railway goods yard near Carlisle, and shortly afterwards a blood-stained jemmy was found at Blencowe in a wagon that had been standing empty in the yard near the location where the two had been seen. The gang were not seen again together during the daytime – they had obviously holed up somewhere, possibly in an empty van.

At around 7 pm the same night the Station Master at Southwaite station, on the main line south from Carlisle towards Lancaster, was approached by a stranger who asked the time of the next train to London. The Station Master told him, but the man said it was too long to wait. The Station Master was rather suspicious and sent for the Railway Police. Then at Plumpton, a few miles further south, the Station Master saw three men acting suspiciously, and he discreetly sent one of his staff to the Railway Police.

Police Constable Byrnes sent a local youth to get assistance, and he then set off to find the three criminals. At about 8.25 pm two men, later identified as Rudge and James Baker, went into the bar at the Pack Horse Inn and ate some bread, cheese and beer. They left after a short time and a little later a shot was heard by the signalman at the station. It was also heard by some other people near the vicarage, then a man passing by on the road heard a low moaning and, looking over the drystone wall, he found PC Byrnes. The constable had intercepted the desperados and they had shot him through the head. The poor man was beyond all help and died shortly afterwards.

The next sighting of the criminals was shortly after 10 pm when a policeman on duty on a bridge near Penrith saw three strangers behaving suspiciously. The bridge was about 4 miles from the Pack Horse Inn, and the constable lost the fugitives in the darkness. However, the search for the murderers was carried on with relentless vigour and a goods train due to leave Keswick Junction, Penrith, for the south was searched thoroughly. The guard of the train, Christopher Gaddes, was told of the situation and asked to keep a look out for anyone acting strangely.

As the train moved off Gaddes saw three men break out of the undergrowth at the side of the line and climb up into a truck. A calm, sensible sort of man, Gaddes acted as if he had seen nothing, but he wrote notes on the back of blank waybills which he threw out of the guard's van as he passed Shap and Tebay. The first was seen by an eagle-eyed engine driver, and a message was telegraphed to Tebay asking the police to meet the train. It will never be known what happened to the message, but there was no police presence when the train arrived, and Gaddes felt that he had been let down. However, at the next signal Gaddes stopped the train and all the available railway personnel were gathered. Armed with sticks, sprags and shovels, they examined every truck, when suddenly the gang leapt out of their truck and a terrific struggle took place.

Martin broke away but the engine driver chased him and grabbed hold of him. He was a vicious man and the driver was badly hurt, but Martin was eventually caught and tied to a telegraph pole. A revolver was found on him. Rudge was also caught after a violent struggle, and he also was found to be in possession of a revolver, and both weapons had been fired recently. Rudge was tied to another telegraph pole to wait for the police. James Baker escaped into the darkness and hid in another railway truck, but near Oxenholme two railwaymen saw him get out of the truck and passed the message on. Later, at Lancaster station, a guard named Cooper saw a man acting furtively moving around the goods yard. This man approached Cooper and said, 'Is this train going to Crewe?'

'Where are you going?' asked Cooper.

The stranger replied, 'Crewe. Liverpool. Anywhere.'

Cooper then challenged him and after a terrific fight Baker was caught, his clothing covered in blood. The other member of the gang, William Baker, was on the bylines of the crime and had no definite part other than in its preliminary planning, but as an accomplice he was sentenced to a period of penal servitude. The other three were taken to Carlisle by train, their arrival witnessed by thousands of people who had heard of the crimes and who wished to see justice done. Feelings were so strong that the Chief Constable and his men were hard put to prevent the three men from being lynched there and then.

The case that had been sent on to Carlisle by Baker was opened with some trepidation, only to find that it contained skeleton keys and other house-breaking tools. Searches of the prisoners failed to find any of the stolen jewellery. However, a few days later a tobacco pouch was discovered in some undergrowth near Tebay station, and it was found to contain all the jewellery except the valuable Diamond Star; this was found later under a railway arch where it had possibly been thrown in panic.

The trial of the three men lasted three days, Mr Justice Day presiding over the Carlisle Assizes on 18-20 January 1886. The jury's verdict was guilty of murder, and Rudge, Martin and James Baker were sentenced to be hanged. The Judge complimented the police and railway staff for their part in bringing the criminals to justice and awarded the sum of £170 to be divided by the authorities as they thought fit.

Rudge, Martin and James Baker kept their appointment with the hangman in the cold, grey early hours of 8 February 1886. On the scaffold Martin admitted that he had fired the shot that killed Byrnes. A memorial was erected to PC Byrnes near the spot where he met his death. Made of red sandstone, it is let into the wall on the road between Plumpton station and the Pack Horse Inn, and bears a cross with the inscription 'Do or Die'.

25
Justice shall be seen to be done!

John Innes Nisbet was a clerk employed by the Stobswood Colliery Company, and it was his duty to pay the wages at the colliery every other Friday. The amount of money concerned varied, but on this occasion he had £370 9s 6d. He usually took a cheque to the local branch of Lloyd's Bank and put the money, which was in canvas bags, into a leather bag which he locked and pocketed the key.

He was noticed by an acquaintance, a Mr Charles Raven, on platform 5 on Newcastle station accompanied by a man whom Raven knew by sight but not by name. Wilson Hepple, an artist, was walking up and down platform 5 waiting for the train whistle to blow and the journey to commence. He had found a seat in the rear of the train when he noticed John Alexander Dickman, whom he had known for many years, pass by talking to another man whom he did not know. They were walking towards the front of the train, which consisted of three compartment coaches and a luggage van.

Two other cashiers, a Mr Hall and a Mr Spink, both of whom worked with Nisbet, were also travelling on the same train to pay wages to other collieries, and they too saw Nisbet walking along the platform accompanied by a man wearing a light overcoat. They also noticed Nisbet open the carriage door and the two men climb in.

It was usual for Mrs Nisbet to meet her husband at Heaton station and have a few minutes' chat. Heaton was the second station out of Newcastle and the train would stop there for a few minutes. On this occasion Mrs Nisbet noticed that her husband was travelling in the front part of the train. When he saw his wife he looked out of the window, but it took her several seconds to reach him. She noticed that he had a companion with him who had on a light-coloured overcoat, the collar of which was partly turned up to hide his face. The train stayed only a few seconds at Heaton as there were no passengers waiting to get on or off.

The train departed on its way to Stannington, and when it arrived Hall and Spink disembarked, Hall smiling a greeting to Nisbet as he passed. Hall noticed, too, that Nisbet had someone else with him in the compartment. The next station on the line was Morpeth, some 2 or 3 miles further, and on arrival a man alighted and handed Mr Athey, the ticket collector, the outward half of a return ticket from Newcastle to Stannington, plus some coins for the excess fare. Mr Athey noticed that he was wearing a light-coloured overcoat, but apart from that he was satisfied that he was just another traveller.

The train took on water at Morpeth, and this took about 4 minutes. A passenger, trying to find a comfortable seat, looked into the compartment of the first carriage, but it was empty. On arrival at Alnmouth, the porter, William Charlton, opened the carriage doors as was his duty, and on opening the door of a 3rd Class compartment of the first carriage an awful sight greeted him – from beneath the seat came a stream of blood, and the body of a man was sprawled across the floor, lying face down.

Further examination showed that he had been shot five times through the head; in fact, two of the bullets were still in his skull. There were signs of a grim struggle; a broken pair of spectacles was found crushed on the floor, together with a hard felt hat that was identified as Nisbet's. A post mortem disclosed that the bullets were different: one was a lead bullet, but the other was nickel-capped. This suggested that two revolvers had been used to kill Nisbet.

The Stobswood Colliery Company immediately offered £100 as a reward for information leading to the arrest of the murderer. The notice ran as follows:

'Whereas on the 17th of March 1910, John Innes Nisbet, a clerk or cashier, late of 180 Heaton Road, Newcastle, was murdered in a third class carriage on the North Eastern Railway between Newcastle and Alnmouth, and a black leather bag containing £370 9s 6d in money (mostly gold and silver) was stolen. A man of the following description was seen in the same carriage as the deceased at Newcastle and Stannington railway stations and appeared to be on friendly terms with Nisbet, about 35 to 40 years of age, about 5 ft 6 in high, about 11 stone in weight, heavy, dark moustache, pale or sallow complexion, wearing a light-coloured overcoat knee-length, black felt hard hat, well-dressed and appeared fairly well to do. The above reward will be paid by the owners of the Stobswood Colliery near Widdrington, to a person other than a person belonging to the police force in the United Kingdom, and not being the actual murderer, who shall be the first to give such information and shall give such evidence as shall lead to the discovery and the conviction of the murderer or murderers.'

Rumours of the sighting of such a person flew around the area. Information was given to the police that John Alexander Dickman had been seen with Nisbet, and Detective Inspector Tait of the Newcastle police called on Dickman for a general chat, hoping for a few leads. During this general conversation Dickman admitted that he had seen Nisbet and had travelled on the same train, but not in the same carriage. When Inspector Tait asked him if he would come down to the police station and make a signed statement, he agreed.

The statement told of his movements at the station, how he travelled at the end of the train, but failed to get out at Stannington as he had originally intended, having booked his ticket to that station. He had not noticed it, so had got off at Morpeth and had paid the excess fare. He had then started to walk back to Stannington, but was taken ill and had to rest for half an hour. After recovering he had resumed his walk and had met a man called Elliot, with whom he chatted for about 5 minutes. He said that the reason for his journey was to see a Mr Hogg at Dovecot Colliery.

There were so many contradictions in the evidence already given to the police that Dickman was arrested for further questioning. The police also searched his house, and found some pawn tickets, a life preserver and two bank passbooks, one relating to an account at the National Provincial Bank and the other to an account at Lambton's (later amalgamated with Lloyds). Also found were a pair of suede gloves on which were bloodstains, but no sign of a gun or guns.

At this stage substantive evidence was proving hard to get. There was circumstantial evidence in that Wilson Hepple knew Dickman well but did not know Nisbet, Charles Raven knew Dickman by sight but he knew Nisbet intimately, and Hall of course knew Nisbet – he worked with him – but not Dickman. Hall identified Nisbet as the man he had seen opening the carriage door, although he only caught a brief glimpse of Nisbet's companion.

The matter became more complicated when Hall was asked to identify Dickman amongst nine other men in an identity parade. He picked out Dickman, saying, 'If I was assured that the murderer was in amongst those nine men I would have no hesitation in picking the prisoner out' – a dramatic statement based on very thin evidence.

The actions of the police were not above reproach in this case, and a letter from the Chief Constable of Northumberland to the Under Secretary of State at the Home Office highlighted the shortcomings. From this letter we are told that when Messrs Hall and Spink went to identify Dickman at the police station, they were waiting in a corridor when it was suggested that they should look through a window of a room that Dickman was in to see if they would recognise him; they could only see the top of his head, as the lower half on the window was frosted. They refused to agree that this was the prisoner.

On another occasion the police suggested to them that they should attempt to identify Dickman through a half-open door. Hall noticed that whoever it was in the room was wearing a light-coloured overcoat, and he *thought* it might be Dickman. The attitude of the police at this stage was not ethical and far from satisfactory; it would seem that they had to get a conviction at all costs.

Dickman was a strange man in many ways. He spent most of his money on the horses, mainly finishing up on the wrong side. His life was strange but not evil; the police had at this stage pretty flimsy evidence against him. Mrs Nisbet, when she was called to give evidence on 14 April, spoke of running alongside the train at Heaton station, trying to have a few words with her husband as she usually did on these occasions. Something strange happened that day in more ways than one: she claims that she swooned as she was running along the platform, and of course when she came to the train had gone, and so had her husband – for ever! To prove that she was not lying, she swooned when she had finished giving her evidence.

However, she claimed that she only passed out when she saw the face of John Dickman. It transpired that Mrs Nisbet had known John Dickman for years, and later she admitted that she had seen him shortly before the murder. Why had she not volunteered that information before? She had every opportunity to tell the police, and the information was crucial enough to have some bearing on the case. Her excuse was that 'she had no cause to do so'. Why did Mrs Nisbet not recognise a man whom she knew well? The evidence of Mr Athey, the ticket collector at Morpeth, who was the last man to speak to him on that fateful day, was that he appeared to a normal traveller, and he had no cause to suspect him of any misdoings.

Going back to Dickman and the firearm or firearms, evidence now suggested that only one revolver was used. The murderer had tried to make the small bullets bigger by wrapping them in paper; this method is not usually successful. A piece of paper was found on the floor of the compartment, but its use had not at the time been realised.

Dickman was in the habit of having letters sent to him under aliases – the name of 'F. Black' was used – and he used a business address in Newcastle for convenience in dealing with his betting transactions. He admitted that a parcel containing a revolver had arrived addressed to his pseudonym, and this was followed a couple of days later by a postcard from the firm asking for it back, as the gun had been sent in error. Dickman collected the gun and postcard and took them away; whether he sent the revolver back is unknown. But still mystifying was the statement by the gunsmith that the two bullets found in Nisbet's skull were the kind that would have been fired from an automatic pistol, and no proof was brought forward that Dickman owned such a weapon. Nor could the prosecution prove anything about the bloodstains on the suede gloves; forensic science was in its infancy in those days.

However, on 9 June an interesting discovery was made when the leather bag in which the colliery wages had been carried was found at the bottom of an air-shaft at the Isabella Pit, a mine 2 miles south-east of Morpeth station, and very close to the road that Dickman would have used when he left the train there. The discovery was made by Peter Spooner, a colliery manager who knew Dickman. Spooner had mentioned the problems associated with working the pit due to the large amount of water, and this air-shaft was covered by a steel mesh grid 6 inches apart, possibly wide enough to squeeze the leather bag through. The bag had been slit but a few coppers were still rattling about in it.

So far the case against Dickman seemed to be circumstantial -his financial position was one big mess, he had held the position of secretary of a colliery syndicate that worked on a variable commission with selected bookmakers, at some time he had an office in Newcastle, and as we know he had two bank accounts. He borrowed money, paid it back, gambled with some, lost it, borrowed more from punters, and kept his wife short; he stayed away from his home for indefinite periods, his poor wife often penniless. His business methods were totally irresponsible, and he pawned everything he could lay his hands on.

So the case against Dickman for the murder of John Innes Nisbet was far from conclusive. If he did commit the murder and steal the money he must have laid his plans very well, for the evidence against him was tissue thin. But in lieu of other substantive evidence in his favour, the circumstances seemed to be weighted against him.

One point of interest is that in 1898 an Act of Parliament was passed stating that the accused person and the husband or wife of the accused may give evidence for the defence, but that he or she could not be called to do so − it was entirely voluntary and entirely at their discretion. In Dickman's case his wife was not called to give support to his defence; he alone stood in the box and tried to conduct his case as regards his own testimony.

In reply to his Counsel regarding why he did not leave the train at Stannington, he said that he had been too occupied reading the

Manchester Sporting Chronicle's opinion of the likely winner of the Grand National, and only the sudden swerve of the train between Stannington and Morpeth made him realise that he was now on the way to Morpeth. Possible. . . Returning to the parcel that was delivered to his pseudonymous address in Newcastle, he stated that he did not open it as he read the postcard that advised him that some mistake had occurred and that the revolver belonged to someone else; he further stated that until he read the postcard he was not aware of the parcel's contents. Again, possible. Dickman agreed that he was wearing an old brown overcoat and not the fawn-coloured Burberry that was described by the prosecution. He also said that perhaps five or six people were with him in his compartment; he had not taken much notice, but they had been there – he certainly was not alone, nor was he travelling with Nisbet.

On balance the prosecution had insufficient evidence against Dickman to hang him, but conversely Dickman's evidence to defend himself was not good enough to protect him from the process of the law. Possibly his wife's evidence might have added some bearing and weight to his case. The jury retired to consider the matter, and many feared that he had lost it. They were right – Dickman was sentenced to hang. He of course appealed – he had a lot of supporters and they were convinced that the evidence against him was too thin, but the verdict was accepted and on 10 August 1910 John Alexander Dickman was hanged in Newcastle Prison.

As a footnote, five of the members of the jury signed the petition for a reprieve. However, it emerged that Dickman was alleged to have shot and killed Mrs Luard, wife of Major-General Luard, at Ightham near Sevenoaks, Kent, on the night of 24 August 1908; this had not been proved, and the allegation had not been mentioned in court.

Today there is no doubt that Dickman would have been found not guilty. Modern methods and techniques would have overturned the prosecution's case. But who did kill John Innes Nisbet, and who ultimately enjoyed spending the £370?

26
'This rotten crime'

On 10 December 1945 a most cold-blooded murder took place in the Station Master's room at Pollokshields East station in Glasgow. This station was situated at a low level, being about 40 feet below Albert Drive, and the only entrance was by means of a long stairway from street level. Between 7.30 and 7.45 pm on that day three railway workers were huddled round the fire talking over the day's events. The weather was cold and icy and they were glad of the warmth from the fire.

Suddenly the door burst open and a man brandishing a revolver ran in and shot each of the three people in turn. Two died but the third, Kerith Scott, the 40-year-old porter-clerk, escaped death by inches and only suffered a graze, the bullet passing through his clothing. The two people killed were a Miss Bradshaw, a clerk who was killed outright, and 15-year-old Robert Brown, who was employed as a junior porter; he was shot through the wrist, the bullet then passing through his stomach. The poor boy lingered on for a day then died of his wounds. Apparently Miss Bradshaw had been shot first, and Brown had tried to protect her. The gunman fired two more shots at her as she lay dying, then fled into the night clutching two empty metal boxes that he had taken from a safe in the next-door office.

The police estimated that six shots had been fired in all, and they were able to circulate a description of the man they wished to interview. Appeals were made to any person who could provide information leading to the arrest of the killer, and to passengers who might have been travelling in tramcars or buses at around 8 pm that night. The appeal extended to drivers and conductors who might have seen a man answering the police's description.

The fingerprint men were busy examining every part of the Station Master's office, while other branches of the law were talking to the survivor, Mr Scott. An appeal was also made to a group of women who were seen walking in a westerly direction along Albert Drive; it was thought that perhaps these ladies might be able to throw light on the identity of the murderer. A man had telephoned the police and had volunteered the information that the women had been in the immediate area and might be helpful.

Young Robert Brown, critically ill in hospital, was able to make a statement to the police, as follows: 'Last night I was sitting at the fire in the Pollokshields East Station Master's office talking with Miss Bradshaw and Mr Scott saw someone passing the window, and the door opened. A man came in with a revolver and pointed it at us. He said, "It is a hold-up." He was wearing a light-coloured raincoat of the kind demobbed fellows are getting, and a soft felt hat. He had a very white face and was clean shaven, his hair was brown and he had light brown eyes. He was about my height. He shot at Miss Bradshaw. I turned to protect her and I fell. He then shot me and ran out of the door. I never saw him again after he had shot me.' He was too weak to sign the statement.

Mr Scott, who was lucky enough to escape the fate of his two colleagues, stated that he had rushed on to the platform and had reported the incident to the guard of the train that pulled into the station. The guard, who did not believe him and thought he was joking, signalled to the driver to proceed.

The patient sifting of information and the interrogation of many people kept the local police very busy, and the search for the killer was spread all over Scotland. Every effort was made to investigate even the vaguest piece of information, and no stone was left unturned, but after some six months nothing had been achieved; apart from the description and a few details the trail had gone cold.

It sometimes happens that when looking for information of a particular kind, other knowledge is gleaned concerning other matters, and such was the case in the police efforts to find their man, for they were able to arrest three other men for possessing firearms. However, there was still no luck in the search for the Pollokshields station killer, so Glasgow Magistrates decided to dangle a 'carrot' in front of anyone who perhaps knew the man and what he had done. They offered a reward of £1,000 to any person who gave information leading to the arrest of the gunman.

About 10 months later the police had a stroke of luck when at 9.50 am on Wednesday 9 October 1946 a Constable Byrne was on point duty in Newlands Road at the junction of Clarkston Road when a young man approached him and said, 'Will you call Central for me?'

'What for?' the Constable asked.

'I did a murder,' the man replied.

The Constable found it difficult to take the request seriously, as policemen meet many odd characters from time to time, and one has to be sure that one's time is not being wasted. So Byrne asked him for some details, and the other gave his name and volunteered details about the Pollokshields station affair. Byrne then recognised the man from the description that he had in his pocket book, and took him to the police box in Spean Street. When they reached the box the man produced a revolver, said, 'You might as well have this', and handed the weapon over with a small box of ammunition. Constable Byrne then cautioned him, and the man said that he had tried to shoot himself but the gun would not go off.

The man was identified as a 21-year-old locomotive fireman from Glasgow, and he was charged with the murder of Joan Bradshaw and Robert Brown. He was also charged with assaulting Kerith Scott and further being in possession of an automatic pistol and 13 rounds of ammunition. At his trial Constable Byrne spoke of a letter that the accused had passed to him, which read: 'Dear Bill, I know you will be very surprised when you hear I have given myself up for the Pollokshields murder. Remember how, on your last leave, we discussed it, but little did you know it was I. I tried to kill myself this morning, but when I pulled the trigger it would not fire, although a little later it fired when pointed at the river. After a while I fell asleep. I woke up knowing I had to give myself up. I hope by this rotten crime have not lost your friendship.'

The letter was addressed to a private in the Highland Light Infantry.

At the identification parade at the Central Police Office Kerith Scott picked out the accused as the man who had fired at him at Pollokshields station. The prisoner was examined by five specialists in mental diseases as instructed by the Defence, and they stated that he was of gross mental abnormality, but was not 'certifiably insane'. They did, however, stress that his condition was separated from certifiable insanity by a hair's breadth, having established that although he had symptoms of strange behaviour, he was, to all intents and purposes, in control of his actions and knew what he was doing. However, the debate as to whether he was sane or insane continued throughout the trial, and the jury was asked to decide the state of the accused's mind when he committed the murders. In view of the psychiatrists' reports it would seem that he could distinguish right from wrong, and the jury would have to take this fact into consideration. The Judge, speaking to the jury, said that there was a motive for the killing, and that was robbery. Dealing with the accused's state of mind, he said that the jury must be satisfied that the case had been made against the accused, that there was also a presumption of sanity, and that it was not for the Crown to prove the accused sane, but for the Defence to prove something in regard to the accused being of diminished responsibility. If the accused had been insane, this would be dealt with under other machinery of law.

Sentence of death by hanging was the Judge's decision on the majority verdict by the jury. But that was not the end, for an appeal was lodged against the death sentence and, amazingly, was upheld, the sentence being commuted to penal servitude for life. Only this strange, confused young man who, from time to time, lived in a world of his own, knew whether he had killed Joan Bradshaw and young Robert Brown in a dream of gun-wielding power, or whether it was violent robbery plain and simple.

27
Ticket to the gallows

*A*nother savage robbery at a station was to occur some seven years later. The former Southern Railway station at Ash Vale, on the Surrey/Hampshire border, was a busy little outpost. One of the BR's smaller stations, it was nevertheless used regularly by the commuters who went to and fro to their jobs in London. As with many smaller stations BR had a system of closing the booking office at 8 pm; the ticket clerk would leave the duty porter a supply of tickets and a date stamp. This arrangement worked very well and the traveller who arrived at the station could still buy and use the necessary ticket.

On the night of 22 August 1952, a few minutes before 8 pm, the ticket clerk handed over some tickets and the date stamp to the porter and closed the office, although he told the porter that he would be staying inside the office to catch up with some work for an hour or two. That was the last time the porter saw the clerk alive.

About an hour later another railway employee saw the light on in the booking office and thought it had been left on by mistake. He knocked on the door and when he got no reply he climbed on to the window ledge to see inside. He saw the safe with its door open and a man's body lying in a pool of blood. The office was in chaos, as if a struggle had taken place. The clerk had been savagely stabbed to death; as many as 20 stab wounds were found to his body and neck, arms and legs. The money from the safe had, of course, gone.

The railway police and the county force combed the area for leads as to the perpetrator of this dreadful crime. They set up an emergency HQ in one of the waiting rooms on the station provided with an emergency GPO telephone line. Searches of hotels and boarding houses were undertaken, and Aldershot, with its military establishments, was also investigated for possible help.

Early in the morning of the next day a soldier came into the incident room at the station to tell the police exactly what had happened while he was waiting for a train the previous evening. He had arrived just before 9 pm and found the ticket office closed. As he made to leave the ticket office area he heard the noise of feet shuffling and the sound of two voices. He then knocked on the ticket office window, and the noises stopped. He then made off to find a porter who would sell him a ticket for his journey. He little thought that he had been listening to the murderer and his victim in the office.

The police had been very occupied with house-to-house searches and their exhaustive investigation had so far seen no results. Aldershot had so far not yielded much in the way of leads until a boarding house was visited by two police officers acting on a tip-off that had seemed vague in the extreme. However, their luck held and in a room on the first floor they found signs of some evidence that they could use – on the bed was a bloodstained jacket, and among the other articles scattered about the room was a wallet and two 10 shilling notes that also had bloodstains on them. The most significant piece of evidence was a passport.

The police stayed at the house for the rest of the day and at around 11 pm the owner of the passport turned up and was arrested. He was found to have a roll of notes amounting to £109, and he showed the police where he kept a sheath-knife up the chimney in a cavity. Also found were some railway documents that he had taken from the safe at Ash Vale station. It appeared that he had been shopping the previous Saturday and had bought a new sports coat, a pair of trousers, and a pair of shoes, obviously to replace the clothes he had worn when killing the ticket clerk. His old trousers were eventually found in some bushes and his shoes were traced to a cobbler in the area.

The man admitted his guilt, the evidence was overwhelming and from the information gathered it appeared that the murder was a planned affair. The accused was a railway fireman and he made use of the fact that he was a fellow railwayman in an attempt to form a relationship with the victim. He was due to go on holiday on Monday 18 August and he had discussed the planned holiday in France many times with his wife. When he left the house on the Monday morning he told her that he was going to collect his holiday pay, but instead of going to the loco shed he went to Aldershot and spent the rest of the week in that area. One can imagine the worry of his poor wife wondering where her errant husband had gone.

The accused appeared at Ash Vale station on the Wednesday morning. He spoke to one of the porters and passed the time of day, then, looking round the station generally, he showed his railway pass to the porter and asked if he could use the telephone in the booking office.

He made a call on the pretext of getting news of an injured signalman who was a mate, then told the clerk that he was expecting a return call with some information about the signalman and that he would come back later. It all seemed normal. Nobody could suspect that a murder was being planned.

On the next day, Thursday, at just after 7 pm, the murderer duly arrived and was told that no phone call had been received. He shrugged off the news and spent nearly an hour talking to the booking clerk. All the time he was planning the crime that would ultimately take him to the gallows.

The next day, Friday, at around 6 pm along he came again, and went to the ticket office. By this time the ticket clerk knew him, and again he asked if he could use the phone. He then sauntered around the environs of the station until just after 7.30 pm, when he once more arrived back at the ticket office and *again* asked if he could use the phone. By this time the clerk was on his own.

The duty porter remembered seeing the other man inside the booking office. The murderer chatted to the clerk in a normal way until around 8.40 pm when he pulled out the sheath-knife that he had bought in Aldershot and brutally attacked the clerk. The poor man put up a determined fight for his life but the other was a match for him and the razor-sharp knife did its worst.

The evidence against the accused was so conclusive that his Defence tried to claim that he was insane, but the Judge and jury thought otherwise and he was sentenced to death for 'this cold-blooded murder'. He appealed against the sentence but this was rejected, and he was hanged in the cold grey early hours of 2 January 1953.

28
Death in the goods yard

*T*his story concerns the violent death of a coal merchant in his premises one dark December day over 30 years ago. Francis Townson rented his coal yard, part of the station goods yard, from the British Transport Commission, as it then was. He was a kindly man who lived in a modest, quiet way, going about his business of selling and delivering coal and coke to the people in the immediate area. His business was long-established and he enjoyed a satisfied clientele.

The story begins on the night of 15 December, a bad night owing to the thick fog that swirled around the street lights. Added to the murk was the corrosive consistency of the fog brought about by the emissions of the heavy industry of the time, with the result that the fog was nearly black and could wreak havoc with anyone with respiratory problems. Mr Townson was seen at around 5.30 pm by one of his drivers who passed £20 over to him, this being the receipts for coal sold off the lorry. Another customer came to pay Mr Townson for some coal. The sum was minor – £1 7s 4d – and had been drawn out of the bank by the customer that day; the serial number of the £1 note was later to be very significant in identifying the stolen money.

Mr Townson's usual routine was to close the business at about 6 pm and go home in his car, which he parked outside his premises. At about 7 pm a railway lengthman, William Walker, was walking through the goods yard after completing his duties as a fog-man, which entailed putting out the fog detonators on the rails to protect the points and signals in the poor visibility. Suddenly the beam of his cycle lamp shone on the body of a man lying close to a parked car; he examined the body and realised that the man was dead.

He informed the police, and the local police surgeon attended the scene, confirming that life was gone and removing the body to the mortuary. The body was identified as Mr Townson, aged 62 years, and the subsequent post mortem found that death was due to the inhalation of blood. However, Mr Townson had suffered serious injuries; his nose was broken, his eyes had been badly bruised and blackened, his cheeks were contused, his brain damaged and three ribs had been fractured. He had been wearing a collar and tie, but another tie had been loosely tied round his neck.

It seemed likely that poor Mr Townson had been attacked from behind, the tie pulled round his neck in an effort to restrain him, then the body thrown to the ground. It was also suggested that when the victim had found the tie tightening around his neck he would have put his hands up to his neck in order to try to loosen it, and had then fallen forward, thus causing his elbows to crack his ribs.

This was clearly a case of Mr Townson's movements having been watched with the plan to steal money. The miscreants would have welcomed a foggy night to spring their trap, though whether they intended to actually kill to achieve their unlawful aims will never be known, for such an admittance would never pass their lips. The matter was treated as murder, and investigations commenced with the interviews of all likely persons who had occasion to use or be in the goods yard during the hours in and around the time of the crime. Many suspects were dragged out of the police files and interviewed, and many a suspect was re-visited by the police and asked for details of their recent movements and whereabouts at the time of Mr Townson's death. The enquiries kept coming back to one man who failed to satisfy certain questions – he maintained that he had been in a pub in the town from noon until 3 pm, and had then left as he had a 'bad back'. He went home and went to bed, where he stayed.

At the time of the crime it is thought that Mr Townson maybe had around £80 in his attache case; this had not been found, and his personal money and wallet had not been touched. The following day, however, the attache case was found floating near the banks of a canal, and some of his papers were also found in the water.

The enquiries progressed patiently, and many suspects willingly helped, but the field was narrowing down once more to the man in the pub. The questions put to him were probing and his tale was not conclusive, but he stuck to his alibi about being in the pub. However, this alibi was rather flimsy and the police visited him again. After hours of questioning he finally admitted that he had been with a mate, and yes, they had attacked Mr Townson, but they strenuously denied trying to kill him. They admitted the theft of the money in the attache case; the man had struggled so much, they said, that he might have got away and raised the alarm – they only wanted the money.

The police knew that they had the right man, and believed the charge should be murder. Once he realised that he had no choice, the man confessed all; he even told where his share of the robbery was, on top of the cistern in his kitchen. The amount they had taken was about £60. His accomplice was interviewed later and also admitted his part in the act; both made statements admitting the attack, but they both denied trying to kill Mr Townson – they only admitted hitting him to stop him shouting for help. The Prosecution, however, believed that, as the result was death in the pursuit of furtherance of gain, capital murder was applicable, and both men were charged as such.

The Defence argued that no evidence of malice was present to support the murder charge, but this plea failed and the pair were committed for trial. The trial opened in the spring of the following year, and the prosecution evidence was not disputed to any degree. Both of the accused gave their evidence, but emphasised that they had no intention to kill. The jury found both men not guilty of capital murder, but guilty of manslaughter. The accomplice was sentenced to 14 years due to the fact that he had been connected with a previous case of robbery with violence together with another person, while the first man received the lighter sentence of 10 years' imprisonment. This was a sordid case of an elderly man being brutally killed for a relatively small sum of money, an instance of the young attacking the old with greed in their souls.

29
The last resort

Turning the clock back to 1881, this story concerns a frightened, desperate man who by circumstance was driven to despair and thoughts of murder to obtain money. Percy Mapleton, alias Lefroy, was a slightly built man; his health had always been delicate, so heavy work was out of the question. He was very fond of the theatre, and the highlights of his life were spent there; he did actually write one or two plays, but they did not achieve much success. He was known as being good-natured, and he had a romantic disposition, hence the interest in the theatre. He also occasionally had short articles accepted by minor weekly newspapers.

Lefroy was no good with money. He liked fine clothes, but they cost a lot of money, and he was always at the local pawnbroker taking in his possessions and receiving small amounts of money to tide him over. Life was hard in 1881, and Lefroy knew it. On 27 June of that year he was almost destitute – he had pawned a small revolver some days before for 5 shillings, and had scraped enough together to redeem the weapon, which he loaded and set off for the railway station at London Bridge, on the London, Brighton & South Coast Railway.

He had enough money to buy a ticket, and he then proceeded to walk up and down the platform looking into the compartments for likely affluent people to threaten with his gun and steal money or valuables. After examining each carriage from the outside, the most likely victim appeared to be an elderly gent who was quietly reading a newspaper.

Lefroy entered the compartment and sat opposite his intended victim. Frederick Isaac Gold was a retired businessman who lived in Brighton; he had kept an interest in a shop in London and every Monday morning he would travel into London to visit Mr Cross, the manager of the shop, who would pay Mr Gold his share of the takings. Mr Gold would sometimes bank the money, or alternatively he might just put it in his wallet and go home. Mr Gold was 64 years of age and he enjoyed living in Brighton where he could relax in comfort, while his trips into London allowed him to call on his friends and former business associates.

On Monday 27 June he had left his home at 8.05 am to proceed by train to London, where he would arrive before 10. He was smartly dressed and carried in his pocket a round pocket-watch with the name Griffiths and the number 16261. On arriving in London he went to see Mr Cross who gave him £38 5s 6d. Mr Gold went to his bank and deposited the £38, then made his way to London Bridge station, arriving at about 2 pm. He had a season ticket and was well known to the station staff. Mr Gold liked a cigar, so he chose a carriage that contained four smoking compartments. He was noticed by the ticket collector sitting in the compartment smoking his cigar and reading his paper.

Mr Gold looked up as Lefroy entered the compartment. Lefroy had a wild look about his drawn face and his eyes burned into Mr Gold as he looked him up and down. The train reached Croydon at 2.20pm, and a few miles further on towards Brighton the line entered the mile-long Merstham Tunnel. As the train raced into the darkness another passenger, named Gibson, heard the sounds of four explosions. He thought they sounded like fog signals.

Several miles further on the train passed the village of Horley, and standing at the lineside talking was a Mrs Brown and her daughter. They noticed that as the train passed them, two people in a compartment were struggling with each another. Mrs Brown thought that they were either larking about or locked in combat. Some 7 miles further on the train passed through Balcombe Tunnel, and after that it pulled into Preston Park station.

As the train slowed to a halt the ticket collector noticed Lefroy by his appearance – he was covered in blood, his clothes were torn and ripped, his collar was missing, his eyes were wild and he looked terrible. One strange thing was a watch-chain hanging from his shoe. Lefroy made out that he had put it there for safety, but when the ticket collector bent down to pick it up a pocket-watch marked with the name of Griffiths emerged. Lefroy was taken to hospital to be cleaned up and his wounds treated, and was eventually allowed to stay with a relation at Wallington, near Croydon.

Meanwhile at 3.5 pm a hat was discovered on the up line, and near a place called Hassock's Gate a young woman working in a field found an umbrella, which was later proved to belong to Mr Gold. Then, at 3.45 pm a platelayer came across the body of Frederick Isaac Gold lying near the entrance to Balcombe Tunnel. It was badly mutilated and a bullet was found in his neck; there was also evidence of knife wounds all over the upper part of the body, and the conclusion was that a long and bloody struggle had taken place between Mr Gold and his assailant. At 5.15 pm another platelayer working on the line nearer Brighton came across a shirt collar, which was later proved to be that of Lefroy. Three Hanoverian medals, which looked like sovereigns, were found in the compartment in which the incident had occurred; Lefroy was in the habit of carrying such medals in his pockets.

As a result two policemen were sent to the house in Wallington, but Lefroy was not there. They questioned the servant and he said that Lefroy had told him that he was going to see the surgeon in the neighbourhood. In fact he did not see a doctor at all – he went to ground. On Thursday 30 June he emerged at the lodging house of a Mrs Bickers in Smith Street, Stepney. By this time everyone was looking for him, so he had given a false name, telling people that he was an engineer from Liverpool. While lodging in Smith Street he asked someone to send a telegram for him; the message was sent in the name of Clarke to a Mr Seal at an office in Gresham Street, and it read: 'Please send my wages tonight without fail about eight o'clock. Flour tomorrow. Not 33'.

Later that day two policemen called at the house and arrested Lefroy; a false beard was found in his room. The evidence against him was considerable, but his lawyers tried to make a conclusive case in his defence. However, the amount of undeniable facts were overwhelming, and the inevitable black cap was draped over the Judge's wig as he sentenced Lefroy to death by hanging.

Two strange letters were discovered while Lefroy was in prison awaiting his trial. The gist of both was that he imagined that he could escape from prison or be able to commit suicide to escape the gallows. They were addressed to a woman named Annie, and he asked her to conceal a saw-file in a common meat-pie, asking her to lay it at the bottom of the oblong tin dish; he also asked her to conceal a small bottle or phial in a cake, which should contain prussic acid which could be obtained from a vet to destroy an animal. This harrowing letter showed the desperate mind of the man. The reply from 'Dearest Annie' was distressing in the extreme: she was praying that he might escape the hangman, she would try anything to save him from this ultimate fate; she knew that they would meet again in Heaven. The letter was full of pity and recrimination, but to no avail. Lefroy was guilty of a vicious murder, and he duly paid the penalty.

The Judge did, however, wonder if Lefroy had meant to commit murder if his victim had paid up without question. If Lefroy had escaped with his loot perhaps the murder may have been avoided. Mr Gold, however, was going to fight to retain his money and belongings, and no wild-eyed little thief was going to get anything from him without a struggle to the death. The mystery of the strange telegram was never explained.

30
The body in the tunnel

Merstham Tunnel also plays a more central role in this story.
Situated on the old London, Brighton & South Coast line near
Caterham, it is about a mile long, and still carries a high volume of
passenger traffic.

Sunday 24 September 1905 was a busy day for the platelayers and
maintenance gang who were working in and around the tunnel. At
about 11 pm the maintenance gang arrived at the length of track they
were packing and tamping and resumed their work after having a break
and their 'snap'. Their foreman was William Peacock. Moving about in
the stygian darkness of the sooty tunnel was dangerous in the extreme;
the oil-lamps cast eerie shadows and did not illuminate the areas where
the gang worked very well. Suddenly the dim light from Peacock's lamp
fell upon a dark shape at the side of the track. Moving cautiously nearer,
he made out the horribly mangled body of a woman – one leg had been
severed, her face had been battered, her left arm crushed. Peacock was
shocked and promptly reported the find to the Station Master at
Merstham station, who sent the details to London as follows: 'Sub
Inspector W. Peacock, while walking through Merstham tunnel, at
10.55 pm this evening, found a female body about 400 yards from the
end of the tunnel. The police took charge of the body and searched it.
No address or ticket or money was found on it, and nothing to show
who she was. The body is lying at the Feathers Hotel awaiting an
inquest.'

The railway authorities thought that it was a case of suicide,
although they did interview over 100 people and had their suspicions
aroused by some of the answers to their questions. However, nothing
happened to change their minds until after what seemed a long time
with no one being able to cast any light on the identity of the woman,
a man came forward and wanted to see the body. After examining the

gruesome sight he avowed the remains to be of his sister Mary Sophia Money, a spinster of 22 years, who lived in Lavender Hill in London and worked at a dairy as a book-keeper. Her brother, Robert Henry Money, ran a dairy farm in Kingston.

Mary Money was about 5 ft 2 in tall, a pleasant-looking girl, strongly built but not coarse-looking. She was wearing a black cotton dress, a floral hat with a pink bow on the side, patent leather shoes and a gold chain around her neck. After considerable questioning Robert Money could throw no light on the circumstances of her death as apparent suicide.

The most interesting discovery was that of a gag in her mouth, a scarf of cotton that had been thrust into her mouth so tight that the police had great difficulty in releasing it. The position of the body at the side of the track suggested that she must have been thrown from a moving train with her arms and legs at full stretch – that would account for the scraping, clawing marks in the soot on the tunnel wall; the hands and feet would have slid down the wall after colliding with it. The impetus would be sufficient to throw her limbs under the wheels, thus severing the leg.

Miss Money had told her friend and workmate Miss Emma Hone that she was going for a 'little walk' and that she would not be long – but she never returned. That would have been at about 7 pm. She called at a sweet shop owned by Miss Frances Golding; she was familiar with the shop as she always called for sweets and chocolate on Wednesdays and Sundays. Miss Golding knew her well, and on that particular day Mary mentioned that she was going to Victoria.

Mary was self-sufficient and independent enough to lead her own life, she was small but attractive, and she had good taste in clothes and would have attracted the admiration of men. In this respect she was very particular and while she had many acquaintances, she was rather reserved; she enjoyed writing letters and also enjoyed mainly her own company. There would appear to have been a complete lack of a regular boyfriend.

The mystery of her strange death deepened until several theories were put to the test. All fell down except one. Mary had told Miss Golding that she was going to Victoria, which meant a train journey; but she had told her friend Emma Hone that she was going for a 'little walk'. One might assume therefore that some kind of cover-up was in process, and a clandestine meeting was to take place somewhere. We may also presume that Mary did go to Victoria, as a ticket collector recognised a photograph of her as the young woman he saw on the station. She was not dressed for a long walk or a long journey, so was she meeting someone at Victoria?

Let us presume that she was meeting the secret man in her life. After the joy of meeting, let us imagine that they walked around for a while chatting and catching up with news; possibly they went into a refreshment booth and he had a beer or two while she had a port or two. They may then have decided to go somewhere on the train; he maybe suggested that a 1st Class compartment would ensure that they had privacy, she giggled and agreed, so they boarded a Brighton train.

As the journey progressed the man, whom the alcohol has give courage and determination, may have become a little too amorous. Not wanting to give way to his entreaties, she perhaps pushed him away, telling him to behave himself. Maybe she started to scream, the man snatched her scarf and tried to gag her, she struggled, tried to protect herself from his arms, kicked him perhaps. At this point he may have lost his temper, and as the train entered Merstham Tunnel suppose he flung open the compartment door and hurled the struggling girl out of the train. Maybe he then dragged the door closed and sat back, trying to calm down as he realised the enormity of his actions. At the next station, which was Redhill, perhaps he left the train. Just a theory.

One more interesting item of information came from a signalman named Yarnley who was stationed at Purley Oaks, north of Merstham; he said that a train passed his box with a man and women struggling in a 1st Class compartment. He glimpsed the man trying to drag the woman towards the door or window. The carriages of several trains were examined closely for any signs of a struggle, but nothing was found.

One final point. Mary Money's brother, Robert Henry, was a very strange man. He was proved to be an inveterate liar and did pass on to the police several contradictory tales, which caused them to waste their time. His career was disastrous, he was no businessman, and led a double life of the worst kind; he lived with a woman in Clapham by whom he had two children, then went off with her sister and bigamously married her after having a child with her. He then went back to her sister. This way of life went on until August 1912 when he began to lose his mind. He took the two sisters and three children to Eastbourne where he had rented a house, then shot all of them, although one of the women escaped, wounded. He covered the bodies in spirit and set fire to them, finally blowing his own brains out. This has no connection with Mary Money's murder, but with the webs of deceit spun by the supposed brother and sister, can we suppose that there was no relationship and that Robert Henry Money was the tall handsome stranger who perhaps hurled Mary Money to her death from the train?

31
Death in carriage No 69

One of the first murders to be committed on a train in the London area took place on 9 July 1864. This infamous deed has been recorded many times, as it illustrates the fact that travelling alone on trains in those days was fraught with danger. Suburban trains shuttled to and fro between Hackney and Fenchurch Street on the North London line, and little did two young men realise that the train that rolled into Hackney at 10.10 pm would begin the mystery of the murder that was to send a German immigrant to the gallows.

This particular train left Fenchurch Street at 9.50 pm for Hackney, the journey taking 20 minutes, allowing two stops at Bow and Hackney Wick. Upon the train's arrival at Hackney, the two young men stepped into a 1st Class compartment. There was just enough light to see that the seats, floor and windows were liberally splashed with blood; on the floor they found a bloodstained hat and under one seat a small leather bag covered in blood, and a walking stick. One of the men summoned the Guard and showed him what they had discovered in carriage No 69. The carriage seats were scuffed and it was apparent that there had been a terrific fight in the narrow confines of the compartment.

What had happened to cause the bloodstains was to be revealed when the driver of an engine running past the Milford Arms Tavern between Bow and Hackney Wick spotted a dark shape by the trackside. Further investigation revealed the body of a man who was barely alive. Badly wounded about the head and unable to speak, he died a few minutes after being found. Letters in his pocket gave his identity as Thomas Briggs, a 69-year-old Chief Clerk of the Lombard Street banking house of Robarts & Company. He was a widower and lived at his son's home in Hackney.

On the day in question he had finished his day's work at the bank and had then gone on to the home of his married niece at Peckham for dinner. Some time later he decided it was time to go home and caught a horse-bus in the Old Kent Road, reaching Fenchurch Street station in good time to catch the 9.50 pm train to take him back to his home.

When the police searched through his belongings in the hope of finding some lead in their investigations, they found that his money, nearly £5 in gold and silver, had been left untouched and a silver snuff box was still in a pocket, but his gold watch had gone; his Albert guard had been ripped out of the vest buttonhole and had broken. His gold eye-glass, which he usually wore with a hair guard, had also gone. The walking stick and the small leather bag found in the carriage were found to be Mr Briggs's property, but the bloodstained hat was not his.

The murder proved a sensation – the railway had become an essential part of everyday life in the capital and fears were expressed that travellers were no longer safe travelling on trains. London's nerve was shaken by this outrage, and would-be travellers now joined groups to protect themselves in the possible event of attack. Things went from fear to farce – if a person entered a compartment alone, however inoffensive and decent-looking he or she may be, they were immediately suspected of being a potential killer, especially if they in any way 'looked foreign'.

The police were baffled and badly needed a breakthrough in their enquiries. The public cry was for the arrest of the foul criminal, and the Government of the day offered £100 reward for information leading to his or her arrest. Posters depicting the hat were displayed throughout London, and the police received a visit from a cab-driver who recognised it, or so he thought, as one that he had bought for a young German immigrant called Franz Muller who had at one time lodged at his Paddington home. Muller came from Cologne, had been in England for about two years, had for a period courted the cabby's daughter, and had worked as a tailor, but his true trade was that of a gunsmith. People who had met him found him handsome and reserved, yet with a friendly disposition. He had often talked about going to America to seek his fortune.

Mr Briggs's watch chain was discovered first. It had been exchanged for another chain in a Cheapside jeweller named Death by a foreigner in his mid-20s, small and thin and talking with a strong German accent. The cabby's daughter showed the police a cardboard box that Muller had given her that bore the jeweller's name.

In the minds of the police, things were now beginning to make some sense. Muller seemed to be their man, but they knew that there was some way to go before they could prove that he had murdered Briggs. When taking out the cabby's daughter Muller had given her his photograph, and when the police showed it to Mr Death he recognised it as the young man for whom he had exchanged the gold chain; he also remembered that the man had an injured leg, which might have been caused by the fight in the train compartment.

Franz Muller must have realised that the police were on his trail, for he decided to make a run for it. He left London in haste for the port of Liverpool where he booked a passage on a sailing ship named *Victoria* bound for New York. The police sent an Inspector and a Detective Sergeant to Liverpool, and they booked their passage on the steamer *City of Manchester*, which was to leave Liverpool on 20 July, five days after the *Victoria*, but which would arrive in New York before the ship carrying Muller. The detectives actually spent 20 days in New York waiting for the *Victoria* to dock. The Inspector carried in his pocket the warrant for Muller's arrest, and when the *Victoria* docked the affair had become common news in New York; at the dockside people congregated to see 'Muller the Murderer'.

Muller neither heard nor responded to these calls, and was astonished when the police came up the gangplank and presented him with the warrant for his arrest and journey back to England. The police searched the box that was his only luggage and inside they found a hat and a gold watch; he had 12 shillings in his pocket. He was formally charged and, after an extradition order had been obtained, he was taken back to England.

The trial in the Central Criminal Court was told by the prosecution that Muller, so intent on going to America, had suffered a grievous blow when he had lost his job. It was alleged that he had looked for Mr Briggs and had found him in Carriage No 69. He had attacked him as soon as the train had left the station at Bow, and during the struggle the old man had fought off the young German as best he could, but was unable to prevent the rain of vicious blows to his head. When he was thought to be senseless, it was alleged that Muller had opened the door and pitched Briggs out on to the track. In the struggle both men had lost their hats, and in the fading light Muller had picked up the wrong one, later removing its former owner's name from the headband and trying to alter its depth.

Muller consistently protested his innocence, and remained calm and composed during the proceedings. His defence counsel, the famous lawyer Sergeant Parry, who had been briefed by the German Legal Protection Society in London, pointed out that the evidence was circumstantial, and cast doubt on the cabby's evidence that the hat found in the train compartment was the same one that he had bought for Muller – how could he be so sure?

Many questions posed during the trial of Franz Muller remained unanswered. It also transpired that Muller had an alibi: on the night of the murder he had visited a 'woman of the unfortunate class' in Camberwell, and someone had seen a man resembling Muller getting on a horse-bus at Camberwell Gate at the exact time that Briggs was on his fatal journey. These revelations were particularly significant as the prosecution could not provide one witness who had seen Muller at Fenchurch Street or Hackney Wick stations, or for that matter on the train at all.

Sergeant Parry's defence was, however, in vain, and the jury returned with a verdict of guilty. Many people disputed this verdict, and the German Legal Protection Society fought on to prove Muller's innocence; they held day-long vigils in a London hotel where they invited anyone who felt he or she could help their cause to come and see them. These efforts were in stark contrast to Muller's letter to his father explaining his dire situation, claiming that he had been framed. His father must have had a heart of stone because he replied tersely that he hoped God would forgive his son if he was innocent and have mercy on him if he was guilty.

The public were fascinated by the trial, and the press had a field day. The question in everyone's mind was, 'Would Muller confess?' – not was he guilty or innocent! The day for the execution was a wet Sunday, the gallows had been erected outside the gates of Newgate Prison and crowds gathered to see the dreadful spectacle. A carnival atmosphere prevailed – all the thieves and pickpockets and card-sharps were there swigging beer, the young gallants, the women of easy virtue, they were all there. Muller was led out on to the scaffold, and as the hangman made the final preparations the Chaplain exhorted Muller to make a full confession, but he repeated that he was not guilty. Finally as he was placed over the drop he muttered something in German: 'Ja, Ich habe es gethan' ('Yes, I am guilty').

Taking into consideration the circumstances at the time, it would have made no difference if he had confessed; his neck would still have been broken or he would have suffocated as the rope tightened around it. Many doubts still remain as to whether Muller killed Thomas Briggs – the evidence was circumstantial in the extreme, and the prosecution's case was certainly not conclusive enough to have hanged him. The murder weapon was never found and exactly how he committed the murder was never established, and for a person who was described by his acquaintances as friendly, warm-hearted and considerate and possessing above-average intelligence, it seems strange that he would commit, in such a crude way, a crime of this magnitude. It seems to me that the case against Muller was flimsy and far from conclusive. Perhaps the strident cries from the people of London led to a scapegoat being found, and possibly caused the law of the land to falter in its administration of justice, committing an innocent man to death.

32
'It's Been a Lovely Day!'

*E*lizabeth Camp was a happy young woman. She had travelled by train from Walworth to Hammersmith to visit her younger sister in the morning, then had caught a train to Hounslow to see her elder sister Ann, arriving just in time for tea. She had chatted happily with her sisters about her forthcoming marriage to the man of her dreams, Edward Berry, who had a fruiter's business in Walworth. Elizabeth was enjoying herself shopping for her wedding.

Elizabeth was a very self-sufficient person. She had started work as a barmaid in the Good Intent in East Street, Walworth, and had learned a lot about the pub trade, but then she decided to take up nursing at Winchmore Hill Hospital for a year or two before returning to the Good Intent as manageress.

The year was 1897, the month was February, and the weather was cold but crisp – quite healthy in fact. Her sisters were delighted to see Elizabeth looking so well and happy, and Ann went to see her on to the train at Hounslow station to catch the 7.42 for Waterloo. Ann and a gentleman friend of the family had taken Elizabeth to a local pub for a celebratory drink, and the time had gone so quickly that when one of them looked up at the clock they found that they would have to rush if Elizabeth was to catch the train to meet Edward. 'It's been a lovely day!' she sighed.

The journey from Hounslow to Waterloo is not a long one and in those days would pass through some pleasant scenery as well as expensive suburbs. It should be noted that in 1897 train travel was not spared occasional violence, mainly no more than robbery and intimidation but unwelcome all the same. Steps had been taken in Parliament to provide 'Ladies Only' carriages, but this had not been pursued.

Edward Berry was very protective towards his Elizabeth, he cared about her safety and used to annoy her somewhat with his fussing; she would chide him and take him to task about his fears for her.

'You'd think I was still a child, instead of a woman of 30 weighing 13 stone!' she would say to her sisters. 'Still, if he wants to fuss over me and it keeps him happy, I don't mind.'

The last her sister Ann saw of her was her laughing face at the open carriage window.

Edward was waiting for Elizabeth at Waterloo as arranged. He had tickets for the Music Hall in his pocket; they both enjoyed the variety shows, then perhaps a little supper. The train Elizabeth had caught at Hounslow was timed to arrive at Waterloo at 8.23 pm. Edward glanced at his pocket watch – 8.23 came, the train drew in, the carriages emptied, but there was no sign of his fiancée. He walked around the concourse, looking anxiously among the disembarking passengers. The familiar figure of his beloved was nowhere to be seen.

Edward had dressed up for the occasion; in his tight-fitting tweed suit and curly Derby hat he looked the tops, and he was sure Elizabeth would have approved of his smart appearance. It was so unlike Elizabeth to have somehow missed the train – she would have telegraphed him if she had known that she would be delayed.

He approached a porter who assured him that the train was dead on time. He was just about to ask the porter the time of the next train in from Hounslow when he noticed a small knot of people gathered round the open door of a carriage. Something seemed to be wrong, and he hurried over. The people were now making gestures, waving their arms and calling for help, then two policeman ran over to the carriage. Edward then knew that something was seriously wrong, and he said to the ticket collector, 'It looks as if they are lifting something out of the train.' The ticket collector made no reply, so Edward took another look and saw the men remove their caps.

'Has there been an accident?' he asked falteringly.

It had been a carriage cleaner who, doing his usual drudge of cleaning out the dust and dirt from the compartments, had found Elizabeth – he had almost tripped over her legs. She was not a pretty sight. She had been thrust, face upwards, nearly under the seat, and a glistening pool of blood spread across the compartment floor.

Poor Elizabeth had been horribly battered to death. She had put up a heroic struggle for her life but her assailant had showed no mercy and had brutally smashed her skull in with a blunt instrument; her face had been torn and bruised, her umbrella had been broken in half as she had probably used it in defence, and there was blood everywhere.

Edward at first could not believe that this broken, mutilated wreck of a human being could have possibly been his beloved Elizabeth. Later on, when he followed the horse-drawn ambulance to St Thomas's Hospital and tried to identify the remains, he realised that his worst fears were correct – the body was indeed that of his beloved bride to be, Elizabeth Camp.

The police mounted a sustained investigation to find any person or leads that might help to find the criminal. No trace could be found of Elizabeth's ticket, and her purse was also missing, but the police said that, with the exception of these items, it appeared that nothing had been taken from the person of Elizabeth Camp.

Scotland Yard, in response to the alarm and unease caused by this vicious murder, sent Chief Detective Inspector Marshall to help the overstretched railway policemen. Marshall had been quick to note that the body was still warm when the train arrived at Waterloo, and that would narrow down the field of enquiry. He reasoned that as the train made stops at Putney, Wandsworth and Vauxhall, the killer must have got on the train at any of these places.

However, intense questioning of the public and railway employees and others in the vicinity at the time produced no results. But Marshall would not admit defeat, and grimly carried on the onerous task. He reasoned that many people would be out and about at that time in the early evening – surely someone would have heard the grim struggle or seen the fight that certainly took place in the confined space of a carriage compartment? As the train stopped at the intermediate stations along the line at 5-minute intervals, it would seem almost impossible that the events could escape the gaze of the local travelling public. Judging by the amount of blood splashed all over the surfaces in the compartment, surely some would have found its way on to the murderers' clothes. Again, one would think that someone would have noticed a man with bloodstained clothes and skin.

Then, came the breakthrough in the investigation. A pestle made of porcelain was found on an embankment at Mount Pleasant, midway between Wandsworth and Putney. It had several characteristic marks – it had a wooden handle, it was 12 inches long and on the part where the porcelain met the wooden handle was the figure 9, but the most interesting part of all was that the pestle had a quantity of human hair and blood still stuck to it. This important find was now sent to Scotland Yard for minute investigation. Unfortunately, in those days forensic methods were not as advanced, and this disadvantage was to result in failure to produce much in the way of benefit to Inspector Marshall.

Nonetheless he arranged for photographs of the pestle to be distributed to the press with the few details that the laboratory at Scotland Yard had managed to find, which turned out to be a number of brass metal streaks suggesting that the pestle had been used at some time as a brass metal mortar. An appeal was put out for all the passengers that had travelled on the 7.42 on that fateful day to report to their local police stations to try and assist the police in their enquiries. There was a good response, but when the police had sorted out all the information, they found little to comfort them or to sustain further investigations.

Then one day a man came forward and said that he had seen a man get out of the train at Wandsworth on the night of the murder. His description was quite helpful: he was wearing a black frock coat and a top hat, he would be about 30 years old and he had a dark moustache. The police issued an immediate appeal for the man to come forward and answer some questions, but only one turned up, a character who said he had committed the outrage and assured the police that he was the man they were looking for. However, it appeared that he was of 'unbalanced mind', lived miles away and never visited the London area.

Rumours galore haunted the case. Scotland Yard had a look at a report that came from the Vauxhall area, saying that a man had been spotted leaving Vauxhall station and had gone into a local pub; he had seemed very agitated, and asked for a large whisky at the bar. It was noticed that he appeared to have bloodstains on his jacket. He drank his whisky, looked wide-eyed at the people staring at the blood on his clothes, and fled into the night. It was a typical story – there was no proof or reason, it was just one of many that circulated in the Waterloo area.

The press was anxious to milk the case for as much as they could get out of it. However, the police did not like being pressurised and seemed to resent the press and the reporters who were everywhere. The case had dragged on too long, Inspector Marshall was under pressure from his superiors to close the case or get a result, and the pestle remained the only real clue that the police had to work on. Patience was running out – someone somewhere knew something, and that person had to be found.

Even Elizabeth's younger sister's husband who lived in Hammersmith came under suspicion. Inquiries revealed that although he was the manager of a large local shop, he was not very well paid; he was found to be living well beyond his means and was heavily in debt to Elizabeth. Could it be that his sister-in-law had demanded some of the money back as she was about to be married? Had he been unable to pay, had a row started, had he followed her to London, getting on to the 7.42 at Putney? Had he found her alone, had there been a blazing row, she threatening to expose his debts and excessive life style, he losing his temper, having brought the pestle along to threaten her? Had he hit her, again and again? Had she fought back like a tigress, breaking her umbrella over his back, he still hitting her with the heavy pestle? Perhaps. To me he seems the most likely suspect; over the years Elizabeth had lent him a lot of money, and under some circumstances he had every reason for wanting her dead – she represented a threat to his job and his future. The police did interview him, but did not find enough to pursue their enquiries.

Instead they interviewed Elizabeth's elder sister's gentleman friend whom had joined in the celebratory drink just before she caught the train. They questioned him thoroughly, but again not enough substance was found to arrest him and he was allowed to go home. He was the last suspect that the police interviewed in the Elizabeth Camp case.

Public opinion was still waiting to be satisfied, but it never would be now. The trail had been allowed to go cold, and Elizabeth's relations and friends showed their disgust with letters to the Police Commissioners, but no good came of it. The Camp case remains unsolved.

Elizabeth was buried in Walworth Cemetery. Her funeral was impressive – more than 150 police, many of them on horseback, followed the black horse-drawn hearse to the parish church of St Peter, an impressive end to a most horrific murder.

33
'I want money!'

George Parker was a very handsome, well-built young man of 23 years, but he had committed varying degrees of crime in his short life, for which he had no regrets. Life for him was one of financial dramas; his use of money was circumspect, but he still wasted all that he earned from time to time. Jobs were hard to come by and he seemed unable to hold on to one; he usually fell out with his employer and his violent instincts, easily roused, got him into trouble on many occasions.

He decided to join the army and see the world, but his unreliable temperament still got him into trouble several times in the couple of years he spent in Her Majesty's service. In the end he was hauled before the Commanding Officer and was given a stiff lecture as to his future conduct. The rigid discipline of army life did not appeal to George, and he yearned for the comparative freedom of civilian life. His last few weeks in the service saw him in more trouble for fighting, and was eventually dismissed as totally unsuited for army life.

He had not been out of the army long before he found himself once again short of money, so he decided to look for a job and found one as doorkeeper at the Lyceum Theatre in London. The money shortage became desperate, and although he was reasonably well paid for that type of job, he found it necessary to rob the ticket office till and disappear. The police were still looking for him when one day in early January 1901 he stepped on to the Southampton to London express at Eastleigh.

He was saying fond goodbyes to a woman on the platform years older than himself and with whom he had begun a passionate relationship. The farewell was such a public affair that people on the platform were shocked by the passion that he displayed towards the woman. 'She seemed too good for him,' remarked one of them. He stepped into the train and sat down. Money was again a problem; he had spent almost the last of it on a revolver, which he was intending to use if necessary to threaten the first affluent-looking person that he met.

Mrs Rhoda King was going to see her sister in Battersea that January day. She lived in Southampton and had left her husband at work and her children being cared for by a neighbour. She was looking forward to a rest on the train and was interested in the fine-looking young man as he entered the compartment at Eastleigh.

Parker's ticket was only valid as far as Winchester, and he could see that he would have to use his wits and threats to get past the ticket collector at Vauxhall where tickets were checked on the outskirts of the capital. When the train arrived at Winchester a third person entered the compartment, Mr William Pearson, a wealthy farmer, well dressed and reeking of solid affluence. The scene was now set, with all the characters in place as the train sped on its way to London.

Parker eyed the farmer. He was sure that he would be wearing a money-belt or a fat wallet, and desperation overcame him. He would have to kill to obtain money, and as the woman was with them she would have to die too. Parker rose, left the compartment, went to the toilet and loaded the revolver. He broke out in a cold sweat – murder was a measure he had considered, but had never reckoned that he could go through with it. Maybe today, as fear and panic gripped him, the thought of the dreadful penalty on the gallows would deter him.

He returned to the compartment. Mrs King was looking out of the window when she heard the noise of the shot and, turning, felt the whizz of the bullet as it passed her cheek on its way to despatching the unfortunate farmer. Seeing Parker with the smoking gun in his hand, she exclaimed, 'My God, what have you done? Why did you do it?'

Parker grimaced. 'I want money. Have you got any?'

Her hands trembling with fear, Mrs King fumbled in her purse. She was splashed with blood from the corpse of Mr Pearson, and implored Parker to spare her if only for the sake of her husband and children. Parker was getting impatient and at last she found a shilling, which he grabbed, then started going through Mr Pearson's clothes. He found his victim's purse and offered Mrs King a sovereign, probably to try to buy her silence.

'Is it any use to you?' he asked.

She shook her head. He looked at her and waved the gun around.

'What do I do with this?' he asked.

Mrs King advised him to throw it out of the window, which he did as the train was passing Nine Elms, beginning to slow down for the approach to Vauxhall. As the train drew into the station Parker had the door open and his foot on the step; as soon as the platform appeared under his feet he leapt off and ran down the platform towards the exit.

He dashed past the ticket collector and thrust his ticket into the startled man's hand.

Mrs King was bawling after him. 'Stop that man, he's a murderer, he's just shot a man!' She staggered along the platform, out of breath and very shocked. Meanwhile Parker was running anywhere to shake off several members of the public who had heard Mrs King's shouts. The police appeared and joined in the chase, and Parker, in his panic, ran down a path to a coke retort house and was trapped by the police, who arrested him.

Mrs King was very upset by her horrific experience, but she had recovered enough to give evidence at Parker's trial for the cold-blooded murder of William Pearson. The Defence tried to establish a plea of temporary insanity, but the jury thought otherwise and returned a verdict of guilty. The Judge pronounced the inevitable sentence of death by hanging, and Parker then confessed his crime, although he displayed no sense of remorse for what he had done. He said that he wished he had killed the heroic Mrs King too, then possibly he could have evaded arrest.

In the cold dawn light of 19 March 1901 George Parker went to the gallows for his misdeed, a sad end to a wasted life.

34
Mrs East's last journey

*T*here have been many unsolved cases of apparent suicide connected with Britain's railways. To 99 per cent of us suicide is completely unthinkable, but as the way to escape problems and adversity the confused, tortured soul can sometimes see no alternative. However, it would seem that a fine line between suicide and murder often cannot be drawn so easily, and the fact that no reasonable solution can be accepted by lack of evidence tends to lead to the Coroner's Court and a verdict of suicide.

The unsolved tragedy of the apparent suicide of Mrs Winifred East, whose headless body was found by the side of the line between Kidbrooke and Eltham, South London, on 14 March 1929, was compounded by the lack of evidence to prove that she had been murdered. Other cases of similar circumstances are described in this book, and the same baffling situations continue to torment the Railway Police in their efforts to bring the satisfactory conclusions that the public demand.

At about 6.10 am on the day in question, a platelayer came across the body of a woman who had been decapitated and electrocuted. She was Mrs Winifred East, the wife of an East London estate agent. The platelayer also found an empty purse near the body, and reported his discovery to the driver of the first train on the line

The doctor who examined her confirmed the cause of death – regrettably this kind of terminal injury was not unknown on the electrified lines, and at first thoughts were directed towards suicide. Then the doctor came across bruises in the kidney area which in his professional opinion had been caused by a clenched fist. This, then, put an entirely new light on the case – Mrs East's death was now being investigated as a possible murder.

The empty purse might suggest robbery. If she had been attacked in a carriage compartment, her assailant might have wrestled with her as she struggled, and pushed her out of the door. In those days it was relatively easy to open a carriage door when the train was in motion. Chief Constable Wensley, who was the first ever CID officer to be appointed a Chief Constable in the Metropolitan Police, and a detective of considerable experience and knowledge, took charge of the case. On 18 March the following statement was passed to the press by Scotland Yard:

'In connection with the death of Mrs Winifred East . . . it is known that the deceased lady entered a first class compartment on the train leaving Barnehurst station at 7.42 pm on Wednesday March 13th which arrived at Kidbrooke station at 7.59 pm. The police are anxious to make contact with all passengers who travelled on this train and who may have some particular reason for remembering the journey. Any information should be communicated to Superintendent Barratt, Blackheath Road police station, Greenwich, SE.'

Mr East was questioned about his wife's lifestyle and their relationship; they seemed a normal, happy couple who seemed in complete accord and a strong bond of trust and understanding was very evident. Mr East said that his wife probably had only £3 or £4 in her handbag when she made the journey.

When PC Rye of the Southern Railway Police met the train at Waterloo he thoroughly examined the compartment used by Mrs East and discovered a number of items jammed at the back of the radiator under one of the seats. These included some envelopes, a Post Office Savings book, a National Savings book, a mirror and a lady's hat that was very crumpled and torn. The odd thing was that there seemed to be no sign of a struggle.

It was very clear now that someone else had joined Mrs East in the compartment, had robbed her, discarded the items found under the seat and had thrown her out of the train. But apart from broken glass in the door there was no sign of violence or damage to the fittings – a complete mystery.

The police contacted Mrs Marjorie Richards, a close friend of the Easts, who said that Mrs East had visited her and they had met at Bexley Heath station on the fatal day. They had returned to Mrs Richards's house and had spent the hours chatting about subjects of mutual interest, as old friends do. After tea they had walked to Barnehurst station where they were just in time for Mrs East to board the 7.42 pm train home. As the train pulled into the station Mrs East had noticed an empty compartment and made for it. She sat in the corner seat facing the engine on the platform side. However, just as the guard waved his flag a young man appeared and jumped into the compartment where Mrs East was sitting. Mrs Richards remembered only seeing his back, but described him as slightly built, medium height, and wearing a light-coloured cap; she estimated his age at 'between 20 and 30 years', and also emphasised that Mrs East was 'perfectly cheerful and in good health'.

Another passenger on the train, a Miss Smallwood who joined the train at Eltham, had some interesting recollections. She and a friend were sitting in the next compartment to Mrs East and they heard screams apparently coming from next door. They also heard the sound of glass breaking, but they thought at the time that the sounds may be due to children playing about. At Kidbrooke Miss Smallwood thought she would investigate the strange sounds; she looked out of the window and saw a man talking to a porter. She later described the man to the police as being between 20 and 30 years of age, medium size, broad shoulders, fair complexion, and wearing a light-coloured cap and a thick overcoat sometimes described as a 'British warm'.

At Blackheath Miss Smallwood had a look into the compartment next to them, but nothing seemed out of place or wrong. However, she must have been rather worried because she said to her friend that she would give the details of the man to the police if necessary. Unfortunately she did not actually pass on this potentially important information.

The Railway Police did their best to examine every piece of information to try and solve this mystery. All the railway staff on duty along the line were interviewed – the ticket collectors, porters, signalmen and ticket office staff. A porter on duty at Kidbrooke said that he had been in conversation with one of the night watchmen when this particular train drew in, and that no tickets had been collected for the train. Therefore it appeared that the person that Miss Smallwood and her friend had seen talking to the porter was this night watchman, who was working on a nearby site and used to come over to the station for his nightly brew of tea. This man came to the inquest, but neither Miss Smallwood nor her friend recognised him.

Likewise, the train staff were not able to throw any light on the circumstances that had led to Mrs East's death. The driver said that the journey was routine and as mundane as always; he had all his work cut out to operate the controls and watch out for signals. The guard had also noticed nothing out of the ordinary, and he told the Coroner that it is quite easy to open and shut a carriage door when the train is in motion.

In the summing up the Coroner suggested that several questions had to be answered. Did Mrs East deliberately open the carriage door and fling herself out? Or was she pushed out by a violent blow to her side? He went on the remind the jury that if someone was so scared as to retreat as far as he or she could, then fall out, it was murder.

The police were not satisfied and pursued the matter for many years without success. We must ask ourselves whether the man seen to join Mrs East in the compartment attacked her or grabbed her handbag, ransacking it for her purse, then hurled the woman out of the open door. The discovery of the documents and personal papers belonging to Mrs East found under the seat seems to suggest that a struggle did take place. Perhaps Mrs East was knocked unconscious when the robber went through her handbag. Or was it a suicide that Mrs East had deliberately planned to look as if she had been attacked then pushed out of the train? Either way Mrs East lost her life, and the sum of money in her purse surely was not the real reason for her death. And a woman attacked in the compartment of a railway carriage does not always have a chance to reach the communication cord. There was even a press campaign to try and find the culprit, but the police drew a blank.

35
The sad case of Arthur Mead

'*I*, Arthur Mead, of 39 Easton Street, High Wycombe, having the fear of death before me and with no hope of recovery, make this declaration. I got on the train at Aylesbury where I went to see my brother-in-law. The man who shot me was not on the train at Aylesbury. Nobody was in the carriage with me. I do not know where he got in. I think it might have been Risborough. There was no argument. He got up from his seat, pulled out a revolver and shot me. I had tried to push him off. He must have been a maniac. He was about 24 or 25, of stocky build. He had on a sort of grey suit and he was clean shaven, wearing a trilby, grey colour. I had never seen him before in my life. I am 52 years of age and I am a butcher. I think it was before we reached High Wycombe that I was shot. It must have been, otherwise I should have got out there. I had a 10 shilling note in my waistcoat. It was all the money I had.'

The dying man tried hard to sign the statement but could not do so, and a few minutes later he died.

The mystery of these strange circumstances began when a passenger in the next carriage to Mr Mead heard a sharp crack as the train entered the tunnel just outside Risborough station, and remarked to the other person in the compartment about the dramatic sound.

The train was the 5.42 from Aylesbury to Paddington, and Mrs Fuller, a machinist, joined the train at Princes Risborough. A few minutes later another sharp crack was heard. Mrs Fuller was puzzled and looked out of the carriage window cautiously to see if a carriage door was swinging open – but nothing untoward was seen. When the train stopped at Saunderton she again looked out of the window, but everything seemed to be all right. However, as she left the train at High Wycombe she noticed a man sitting in a corner of the compartment next to hers. She noticed he seemed to be slumped in the seat as if he was asleep.

The year was 1936 and the month was February. The Great Western Railway was in its heyday, proud of its high standards of timekeeping, cleanliness and general respectability. The staff were hand-picked, chosen for their manners, hard work and smart appearance. 'God's Wonderful Railway' was a happy nickname.

The train that Mrs Fuller travelled on was worked by Guard Phipps from Aylesbury to High Wycombe and by Guard Wood from High Wycombe to Paddington. As the train drew into High Wycombe, Wood was ready to take over the duties and he walked the length of the train looking into each compartment. He found 25 passengers in all, and in a corner seat of the Brake 3rd he found a man apparently asleep. He looked haggard and ill, and a few minutes later Wood told the booking clerk that he had found this passenger looking far from well. They discussed the situation and Wood told the clerk to have the ambulance cabin ready.

As the train continued its journey to Paddington, Wood was getting very anxious and stayed with the man until they arrived at Beaconsfield. He noticed that saliva was running out of his mouth. Wood then asked him if he was ill. The man mumbled 'No'. Wood then enquired as to where he was going. The man, with an effort, answered 'High Wycombe', the station they had just left. Guard Wood was getting very worried about the man's condition, and with the help of a porter carried him from the train to the Beaconsfield waiting room. He then locked the compartment from both sides as a customary precaution.

While awaiting the doctor, Porter Bingham administered some first aid to the sick man, and to his surprise the man suddenly said, 'A man shot me with a revolver'. He then lapsed into painful silence. Dr Kipping arrived at 6.45 pm and carried out a very through examination of the man. He found evidence of a gunshot wound on the left-hand side of the chest below the heart, with the exit wound on the fellow's back three inches lower down.

The man regained consciousness during the examination and gave again in halting words that were clearly difficult the information that he had been shot. The doctor phoned this information to the county police, and shortly after Sergeants Jennings and Foster arrived at the station. Dr Kipping told them, 'This man is in a very serious condition. He has been shot through the abdomen and he cannot be expected to live very long. He states that he was shot by a strange man when travelling on the train.' Sergeant Jennings asked the man a few questions. He gave his name as Arthur Mead of 39 Easton Street, High Wycombe. He said he was travelling on the train from Aylesbury when a man got in at Princes Risborough, pulled out a revolver and shot him.

He gave a short description of the assailant as being dark, about 24 or 25 years, short, thick built, wearing a grey trilby and a grey suit. Sergeant Jennings telephoned this information to Paddington and then spoke to Dr Kipping, who then said to the dying man, 'Your condition is very serious and you will die very soon. Do you understand?' Mead replied, 'Yes'. He was then asked if he wanted to make a statement, and he proceeded to tell his story of the events that were to cost him his life.

The two police officers were with Mr Mead when he died shortly after giving the details of the incident, then the full power of the law swung into action. Detective Sergeant Griffin met the train at Paddington and the compartment was searched in minute detail. They found a copy of the *Times* newspaper in the gangway dated 3 February 1936, but they could find no sign of a struggle in the compartment. On removing the seats on the side that Mead was sitting, however, one important development occurred. Sergeant Griffin came cross a spent bullet. It was found resting on the frame board at the rear of the seat, a small dent in the woodwork about eight and a half inches from the cushion level and 18 inches from the window. All these facts were consistent with the possibility of a man being shot from the front when seated.

The fingerprint and photographic department arrived soon after and again inspected the compartment in microscopic detail. Sergeant Griffin told them of his findings.

Arthur Mead's body was examined by Detective Sergeant Rawlins for the county police. His clothing consisted of a medium weight overcoat, jacket, waistcoat, shirt and vest. They found clear signs of a firearm having been pushed against the overcoat – the cloth was burnt and a faint circle marked the spot where the muzzle had been hard against the cloth.

The circumstances seemed to indicate a certain aura of mystery. The question in most people's minds was where was the weapon responsible for the crime, if that is what it was? Suicide hadn't been ruled out at this stage.

In view of Mr Mead's statement many enquiries were made at all levels at Paddington. Much of the station had been closed to allow uninterrupted investigation, but no one answering the description given by Mr Mead was found.

Early next day an exhaustive search was made of the line and, as luck would have it, a ganger came across an object lying on the ballast. It was some sort of gun. The ganger was puzzled as he hadn't seen anything like it. The smell of powder was still apparent and the weapon was identified as a humane killer. Mr Churchill, the well-known firearms expert, was shown the gun and after careful examination he confirmed that the bullet that killed Mr Mead had come from the humane killer.

Also it was thought that the weapon had been thrown from the window of a London-bound train.

Sir Bernard Spilsbury, the eminent pathologist, made a post-mortem examination of the body and said that the bullet fired by the humane killer had produced the fatal injury and that the weapon must have been pressed close to the body of Mr Mead.

Mrs Fuller's statement that the fatal shot had been fired between Princes Risborough and Saunderton seemed to fit, but what caused the second loud crack, identical to the first? No other bullet was found in the compartment. Did Mr Mead commit suicide? And if so, what a dramatic and horrific way to do so. Also, did he have enough strength to rise from his seat and lower the window to hurl the gun out of it?

Enquiries were made about his private life and background. His wife had known him since they were children together. He was a butcher by trade, but for the last few years he had been working in a knacker's yard. He had served in the Army during the First World War, and subsequently his health had suffered badly. He had been receiving hospital treatment, and his nerves were so bad that his doctor had recently recommended that he should be treated in a mental hospital.

He owned two humane killers, the old bullet type now replaced by the captive bolt type. One of these guns had been passed on to his brother-in-law, but he had kept the other and Mrs Mead thought she could safety say that the gun found in the ballast was her husband's.

No one answering the description of the man given by Mr Mead was ever found, so who was he and why should he want to commit murder, if that is what it was? Mr Mead had no known enemies. The landlord of the White Lion at Waddesdon had known the dead man since 1919, and when he last saw him he was trying to raise some money. He even asked the landlord to lend him a few pounds.

It was beginning to suggest that Arthur Mead had committed suicide, but his last words, that a man had got on the train and had shot him, were so clear. Did Arthur Mead die with lies on his lips?

The inquest at Beaconsfield on 29 February 1936 returned a verdict that Arthur Mead took his own life at a time when he was not of sound mind, a verdict not entirely conclusive to many people. The one unexplained fact was that *two* shots were heard, but two bullets did not strike Arthur Mead and the second bullet was never found. But he died with that clear statement on his lips. Not many people would pass on with an untruth at the end. He must have had quite a struggle with his conscience to die like that.

Will anything ever be found to challenge the coroner's verdict of suicide? Will the man so clearly described by Mead ever by identified?

36
Mademoiselle est mort

*A*nother unsolved mystery that still lies in the files awaiting more evidence to bring the incident and the unfortunate death of a 17-year-old schoolgirl to a conclusion has the railway police baffled, but not without hope of more information. For the movements of this French schoolgirl, daughter of a French nobleman, are very much clouded by mystery.

A happy-go-lucky and lively girl, full of life and youthful vigour, she took life in her stride and was popular with her fellow pupils and teachers. However, her life was to end in extreme violence, throwing the Railway Police into confusion as they tried to piece together her last movements. On a January day some years ago a young, attractive girl of some 17 years disembarked from a cross-Channel steamer at Southampton. She was returning to her school in the Midlands, where she was in her last term, and while she enjoyed school life and her good friends, she was looking forward to leaving, and, in her own words, 'having a good time'. A friendly member of the ship's crew helped her with her heavy suitcase and was impressed by her grateful smile and friendly manner.

She had intended to catch the 12.15 pm train from Euston, but somehow she missed it. There were further trains at 1.30 pm and 2pm, so she sent a telegram to the school asking them to arrange for a taxi to meet her at 5.20 pm at the station nearest to the school. She had obviously decided to travel on the 2 pm, leaving almost two hours to spend at Euston. She was seen talking to at least six people on the station – was she asking questions about the train that she had decided to take back to her school? Or had she met a good friend? Or was it just her friendly, open personality that craved the company of like-minded people?

She was then seen talking to a woman in a most animated way near the carriage door that she was to use to climb aboard the train, and she seemed to be in a very uneasy mood – her agitated demeanour had been very apparent to a ticket collector. It was very uncharacteristic for her to react in this way unless she had been frightened by the conversation with the woman. Just before the train left she was seen to be looking out of the window up and down the platform as if looking for someone. That would seem to be the last anyone saw of her, or the last occasion on which she was seen by anyone who was prepared to admit to seeing her at Euston anxiously scanning the platform looking – for whom?

The taxi duly turned up at the station to await his passenger. The train arrived and some people got off and made their way through the ticket barrier to their cars or buses, but there was no sign of the young lady that the taxi-driver was to meet. He waited a few minutes, then got out of the car and asked the station staff if they had seen a girl get off. They shook their heads, and the driver, non-plussed, got into his taxi and drove off.

Little did he know that when the train had pulled into Rugby, where the girl should have changed, a carriage door had been swinging open and there had ben no sign of the young woman. On the floor of the compartment a lady's handbag had been found; that was all. The line was searched immediately, and about three hours later the mutilated body of the French girl was discovered in a tunnel a few miles from Rugby and some 81 miles from Euston.

The body had been terribly mangled and it was almost impossible to ascertain whether she had fallen frontwards from the train or whether she had been pushed or thrown out of the door. There appeared to be no evidence of theft – her purse and jewellery were still intact. An accident seemed very improbable as the carriage door had a double locking device that prevented it from opening accidentally while the train was moving, and the door was known to be closed when the train had left Northampton.

The question of suicide arises, but bearing in mind the happy, outgoing nature of the young woman, this conclusion is unlikely. But as we do not know what effect the conversation at Euston with the other person had on the girl immediately before the train departed, is impossible to draw a conclusion. Had she been badly frightened by a threat? Had she agreed to meet a friend who never turned up? A boyfriend, perhaps? Clearly something or someone had stirred up her emotions that day – after all, she could have taken the earlier train back to school, but instead had chosen to take the 2 pm. We are left with very few clues or tangible ideas why this happy teenager met her untimely death in such a dreadful manner.

The most improbable reasons are in some cases found to be true, and in this case one can only guess. Her family were as puzzled as anyone by the strange circumstances of her death. They knew of no reason why she should have been threatened by a stranger, or why she had not have taken the 1.30 pm train back to school; she was still subject to school discipline and possible insistence by the Principal might have persuaded her to resume her journey back to school without delay. It would seem that the young lady clearly had a mind of her own, but that, while still a pupil, albeit a senior one, she should still observe the regulations that bound her to the school regime. Such abdication of responsibility and her decision not to return on the earlier train apparently cost her life in the most horrible way, and caused her parents and friends the worst heartache.

The British Transport Police left no stone uncovered in trying to ascertain the reasons why the life of a happy, popular girl had been taken in this savage way, and the identity of the unknown criminal whose act may have caused it, but to this day the case lies unsolved in the police files.

37
The lost hours

*T*his story is similarly mysterious and very sad one, and concerns the death of a young woman of 20. On a June evening a few years ago the girl's body was discovered beside the main line by the driver of a freight train, who reported the finding to Control.

Subsequent expert medical examination of the body revealed injuries consistent with a high velocity impact such as falling from a speeding train, and at this stage it was not thought that foul play could be involved. The pathologist's report was that death caused by a fall from a moving train was an acceptable conclusion. However, every effort was made to explore other possibilities and an incident room was set up at the station near where the body had been found to investigate further the circumstances of the girl's death.

The victim was a creature of habit whose daily work routine as a typist with BR was of a high standard, and an irony of this story is that on the very day of her death she had been promoted. Her work gave complete satisfaction and she was popular with her colleagues. Being a BR employee she was entitled to free or privileged travel, and she had a free residential pass between her home and her place of work. Her routine was simple: she always used the 8.06 am from her home station in the morning, and returned on the 5.15 pm in the evening. In the morning she would accompany her father, who also worked for BR, on the walk to the station, then leave him and travel into town with her friends. In the evening she would travel on the train with her friends and rejoin her father for the short walk home; it was a good arrangement that was fully understood.

But there was no apparent reason for her to have been on a southbound main-line train that night. Inquiries were made to trace the actual train she had been on. There were two possibilities, and both trains were taken out of service and put through a thorough examination. The police were looking for human remains, and the carriage doors were also examined to check for faulty door locks that might have opened if leaned on in any way; however, the result was negative. On one of the trains the buffet car door had a fault, but it was not of the kind that would cause it to swing open accidentally.

Many enquiries were made of drivers who regularly passed the place where the body was found, but none had seen it except the driver who had initially reported it. The light on that evening had been good, and the position of her body and colour of her clothing suggested that her body would have been seen by other drivers. It was therefore assumed that she had travelled on the later of the two trains, and this was largely confirmed by certain people who worked with her in the same office. It was then decided to try and trace as many as possible of the passengers and/or railway staff who had been on that train and, to play safe, to also trace anyone who had travelled on the earlier service.

This exhaustive task lasted some five weeks as police officers travelled on these trains every Tuesday night. They managed to interview everyone who had travelled by the route in question, and posters appealing for information were displayed on all intermediate and surrounding stations. Appeals were also made on television, radio and in national and provincial newspapers. No stone was left unturned.

Tests were carried out at BR's Technical Centre at Derby that simulated the same speed at which the train had been moving that night, which was thought to have been around 75 to 80 mph, and these proved that it was possible for anyone to open a carriage door even *against* the direction of travel to effect an exit. Inquiries revealed 28 passengers who had travelled on the earlier of the two trains, and 71 other passengers together with school parties who had been on the later one. The staff at all the intermediate stations along the route were interviewed but no positive sightings of the girl had been made. However, one person on the second train said that he had heard a 'bump' from the outside of the train near where the body was later found – whether this was of any significance was not immediately clear. The railway staff at the station near the sight of the grim discovery assured the railway police that all doors on the platform side of the later train were closed and secure on arrival and departure.

It was found that none of the girl's friends could give any idea why she was travelling south that day; it is inconceivable that she could have taken the train in error, as her habits were such that the routine was so much ingrained that she and her friends always travelled together. Moreover, the train on which she was thought to have travelled left from a different station from that at which she caught the suburban train; the stations were in completely opposite directions from her place of work. When she spoke to her friends about her promotion, she seemed happy and relaxed about the future, and on the evening of the day before she died she arranged with her best friend to meet at her home the following night. Certainly the world seemed a happy place for the girl!

The following day, the day of her death, she followed the old routine: the walk to the station with her father, the meeting with her friendly travelling companions and the journey to work – it would appear to have been a perfectly normal day. During her lunch break she chatted with her friends in the office; they described her mood as relaxed and apparently happy. But at about 4 pm she had a visit from one of her friends in the typing pool who somehow thought she was showing some signs of worry; she complained that she had a lot of work to do as one of the other girls was off sick. Things were certainly busy in her office – so much so that she was asked to stop on to assist her boss, who was talking to an important client. She telephoned her mother to warn her that she would be a bit late home, so that her mother would not worry about her safety. She took tea and biscuits into the office and at about 5 pm asked her boss if he needed her further. He told her to pack up and go home as he could manage, and from this time onwards things get very vague.

Her routine had been broken. If she had caught her normal train and travelled home with her friends she might be alive today. Numerous enquiries were made about the possible route she would take from the office to the station, but these proved inconclusive. Incredibly, a neighbour reported having seen her walking down along the road towards her home between 5 and 5.30 pm; the neighbour stressed that she had pointed out the girl to a friend. If this information was true, and she was within 100 yards of her home, how did she get back to town and why did she decide to travel south? The neighbour was closely questioned by the police and gave her consent to be questioned under hypnosis, she still said that she had seen the girl on the evening of her death. However, house-to-house enquiries failed to reinforce her statement, and other probes included interviewing taxi-drivers, station personnel and car owners at her office, but they all drew a blank. The guard on the later of the two trains train also volunteered to be questioned under hypnosis, but he was unable to help.

The question remained – where did the lost hours go? Why did the girl decide to travel south? Had she committed suicide as a result of anxieties at work? Had she some disturbing dark secret that made her jump to her death? Or had she a secret tryst with a demanding friend? Was she pushed out of the carriage door? Her friends were adamant that she was completely trustworthy and reliable, and she often spoke excitedly about her sister's forthcoming wedding, when she was to be a bridesmaid.

So far the case remains unsolved. Perhaps time will one day reveal the answer.

38
Murder on the 9.02

One day in early spring a few years ago, a 35-year-old woman boarded a train to travel to London to meet her husband so that they could keep an appointment with a specialist in connection with injuries that she had sustained in a car crash a few years earlier. The couple had been married for several years, but had to travel extensively in their chosen jobs; this meant that they spent long periods of time apart, so much so that they had, by mutual consent, agreed to part, albeit on the most friendly terms, and they got together as often as they could.

They met at around 10.15 that morning and went to see the specialist. Following the consultation they decided to spend the rest of the day together, and had lunch in a nearby restaurant. After a leisurely meal they went to the West End and bought tickets for the film *A Passage to India*, then on leaving the cinema they took a taxi to the main-line terminus where the wife collected some presents for her husband's birthday that she had left there when she had arrived that morning.

As there was time to spare they went to the terminus from where her husband would catch his train home, and looked round the shops there. He boarded the 8.35 pm train, and his wife waved to him until the train disappeared from sight. Their farewells had been happy and sincere; they seemed to have enjoyed their day together.

She had told her husband that she intended to catch the next available train home, and it was decided that she should get a taxi. She checked her money in her purse and found that she had at least £15. Allowing for the journey in the taxi between the two stations at that time in the evening, it appeared that the next available train would be the 9.02 pm stopping train. She probably did not realise as she stepped into the train that a few minutes later she could have caught a non-stop straight-through service.

Later, at about 11.10 that night, a passenger stepped aboard the second carriage from the front of the 9.02 and immediately noticed a large pool of blood on the floor and on the seats, so much so that it had run down the centre aisle in a forward direction for about 12 feet. Some 20 minutes later, another passenger boarded the same carriage a few stations later, and the two of them discussed this disturbing situation. They arrived at the same conclusion: that someone had been severely injured or murder had taken place in the very carriage where they were sitting. At the next stop the two men called a British Rail Chargeman over and showed him the sight of the blood. The latter undertook to alert the railway police when the train reached its destination in a few minutes time.

The police duly met the train and when they saw the bloodstained interior they took the train out of service. It was very obvious that something very serious had happened, but there was nothing to go on until they found either a badly injured person or a bloody corpse.

The driver and guard who had worked the train were seen and questioned but could offer no help; they had seen nothing. A British Transport Police Officer was detailed to travel on the 00.15 am train to search the line for any sign of evidence that might give some explanation of the mystery of the blood in the second coach of the 9.02.

The answer to their questions was found some 50 miles down the line near a road bridge, where the body of a woman was found lying between the rails of the southbound track, her face and neck covered in blood. The civil and transport police were soon on the scene, and it was decided to set in motion a joint general investigation into the reason and motive for this murder, for that is what both forces agreed it was.

A senior police surgeon examined the body at the scene and confirmed the cause of death; he was certain that the woman had died of a stab wound in the throat, and that she was dead before she was thrown out of the train. In the area where the body was found a lady's handbag with bloodstains in it, a bloodstained woollen glove, a pen and a red bead were found. The handbag had no any money in it, and the bloodstains could have been those of the assailant rather than the deceased. The two rings were missing from the hands.

The police search was meticulously thorough, the search for forensic evidence extending for a distance of some 30 miles along the track. Various items were found and identified as some of the victim's personal effects, which had been thrown out of the train at intervals. At this time, however, the actual identity of the body had not been finally confirmed; only when her husband and father came to the morgue were they able to confirm her identity. Up to then only a photograph found in her handbag, which had been taken years ago, was available.

A post-mortem examination revealed that the deceased had sustained a stab wound to the left-hand side of her neck that had severed the jugular vein, and this, together with wounds to other parts of her body, had brutally killed her. During the detailed examination of the carriage by BTP officers, traces of palm impressions were found on the door window, blood on the floor carried a footprint of a size 8 baseball boot made in either Hong Kong or Korea, and the left foot imprint suggested that the killer had a bad limp. The police had no doubt that the murder took place on the train and that the body had been thrown from the train.

Murder on a train always attracts the media's interest and this case proved to be no exception. To try and contact people who might be able to help them with their enquiries, the police embarked on a reconstruction of the case. A local housewife dressed in identical clothing to the deceased took her place on the 9.02 pm train a few days later, and extensive enquiries were made to trace members of the public or British Rail staff who had travelled on that train on the night of the murder.

From their investigations it would appear that the victim had been seen by a man who had been on the platform when the train arrived at one of the stations along the line, and he clearly saw two people in the second carriage, a man and a woman; the woman was looking out of the window. As a result of their enquiries from passengers and British Rail staff, the police received reports of many suspicious characters, and all this information was monitored and evaluated.

As a result one particular character became the subject of the police investigation. He was a man who had first been sighted getting into the victim's carriage; the same man was later seen acting suspiciously when the train arrived at the station just before where the body was discovered, and was observed later by witnesses after he left the train at a station beyond that spot. He was described as a young person, quite tall, with blond-streaked collar-length hair, which gave him the appearance of a woman, wearing a jacket, old-fashioned flared trousers and white baseball boots; he was carrying a radio/cassette player and walked with a pronounced limp.

He was first noticed at an intermediate station just after 9.15 pm when he was observed going to the left luggage lockers to remove the radio/cassette player; he had a walking stick and was limping badly. A witness saw him on the platform, and when he hauled himself on to the train the witness noticed that he got into the same coach as that occupied by the woman; he enquired of the witness the destination of the train.

When the train arrived at the station near where the body was found, two postal workers noticed two people in the second carriage – one was a woman sitting next to the window, and they could not help noticing that she sat absolutely motionless; she seemed almost to be propped up in the window seat. The other person was a man who opened the door and stepped on to the platform; he still held on to the door, and at first the postal workers thought he was a woman, but realised it was his long hair that gave that impression. They remembered the glazed look in his eyes. Just before the train left he climbed back into the coach and pulled the door closed.

A couple of stations later he was seen to leave the train by a railway worker; he lurched up to the railwayman and asked about the next train to Scotland. Another passenger on the station got into conversation with the suspect, and the man played one of his tapes in the waiting room. A man and his girlfriend also noticed the young man with the limp, and they noticed the blood stains on his clothes. The young man gave the first witness a £10 note and asked him if he would get him some beer and sandwiches; he bought eight cans of lager and a few sandwiches, and they proceeded to consume them on the northbound train. The witness could not help noticing the bloodstains on the young man's clothing and asked him what had happened. The reply was that he had fallen through a window, and when the train arrived in Scotland the two parted.

On receipt of this and other information, the police checked the local police information centre for any news of criminals or suspects that might have been taken into custody or had some connection with Scotland. This intelligence exercise paid off, and it was revealed that a 15-year-old Scottish boy had visited a local police station one afternoon two days before the murder to answer bail, having been arrested earlier in the year on suspicion of burglary; as that enquiry could not be finalised at the time, he had been 'delay charge' bailed.

This information was helpful and more details were sought from the police locally and in Scotland to trace the tickets that may have been used. The search at the departure station revealed that same day two forward halves of 2nd Class tickets issued in Scotland had been collected. Searches through some 3,000 tickets at last found the return half of one of the tickets, which was found to be bloodstained. Further enquiries discovered that the two tickets had been issued to the suspect and his father to attend for the 'delay charge' bail.

At 7.30 am on the day after the murder the suspect turned up at the house where his father was living. The owner of the house noticed the young man's bloodstained clothing and asked him where the blood had come from. The boy replied that he had got into a fight with three Pakistanis in London, but she did not believe him; his clothes were covered in blood, he appeared to be very frightened and was suffering from shock.

His father, who was still in bed, came down to see his son who told him that he had been in a fight when three Pakistanis had tried to steal his radio/cassette player from him; he said that one of them had a knife and he had been cut, and that accounted for the bloodstains.

'You look as if you have committed a murder,' said the woman, little realising that he had done just that. She did not like the look of the situation, so she asked the man and his son to leave the house, and they moved back home.

One afternoon a week later four police officers representing both English and Scottish forces arrived at the house where they saw the suspect and told him that they were making routine enquiries about a murder on a train the previous week. The young man agreed that he had been in the area and he admitted that he had returned to Scotland by train; he also agreed that he had used a walking stick because of a knee injury. The police asked him to accompany them to the local police station, which he did voluntarily. At the station he admitted that he had travelled in the same carriage as the victim, then he proceeded to lie. His first story was that two coloured men had got into the coach and started pestering the woman, and he had gone to her assistance; in the fight that ensued they had knocked him out, and when he came to there was no one in the carriage and he got off the train.

When he had finished giving answers to their questions he broke down and cried, and said that what he had just told the police officers was untrue and that the woman had jumped out of the moving train. The suspect was then seen by two other officers, and after further intensive questioning he admitted that he had stabbed the woman in the neck while trying to steal her purse. He told them where the attack had taken place and that the knife he used was the one that was recovered from his home. He went on to say that he only wanted to rob the woman, certainly not to kill her.

Forensic evidence showed that the knife wound in the neck would have paralysed the victim, and that she literally bled to death. Her assailant had then dragged the bleeding body to the door of the coach and pushed her out on to the track. He then threw the items of jewellery and other articles out on to the track at intervals.

At his trial he was charged with murder, but he pleaded not guilty, his Defence claiming that he was under the effects of the drug LSD and was not responsible for his actions. At a second trial he again pleaded not guilty, but after the jury had heard the evidence he was pronounced guilty and sentenced him to be detained during Her Majesty's Pleasure for this callous and evil murder.

39
The riddle of the
black trunk

*B*lack cabin trunks left in cloakrooms on railway stations tend to attract an aura of mystery because of tales like these ones that follow. Surely they *have* to contain the bloody remains of a human body or something equally horrifying and sinister! On Tuesday 10 May 1927 it was reported that a black trunk that had been left in the cloakroom at Charing Cross station had been opened and inside was the dismembered body of a woman. Unfortunately no one knew the date or time that the trunk had been brought to Charing Cross, and the condition of its contents suggested that the murder had taken place some while ago.

The fact that there were markings on the trunk did help to start the investigation – the letter 'A' was painted at each end and the initials 'I. F. A.' were marked on the lid, while a tie-on label was addressed in large letters to 'F. Austin, St Leonards'. Amongst the blood-soaked clothing was an article marked 'P. Holt'; another was marked with the faint, blurred numbers 581, and another the faint laundry mark 447. Mr F. Austin was quite easy to find in St Leonards, and was helpful insofar as he proved conclusively that he had nothing to do with the crime, so that lead had been dealt with.

The newspapers had been given photographs of the trunk and direct enquiries were made as to where one would buy such an article second-hand. The press's co-operation soon brought some information. A family named Holt who lived in Chelsea contacted the police, as at least one of the bloodstained garments in the trunk belonged to a Miss P. Holt. Although she was alive and well, her mother was able to identify the body as a cook who had worked for the Holt family briefly. The name that the cook gave the Holts was Roles, and they were certain that there was a Mr Roles.

The police then directed their efforts to find Mr Roles, and shortly afterwards he was found and interviewed. He, too, was quite helpful – the murdered woman had lived with him and had used his name but she was not his wife. They had quarrelled and she had left. The police were satisfied with his story and turned their investigations to try to find out more details of the dead woman.

A young girl volunteered the information that the woman's name was Mrs Minnie Bonati and that she was the wife of an Italian waiter; the man was found and stated that they had parted years ago and he was able to satisfy the police regarding his information. The police were now able to discover more details about Minnie Bonati. Her husband identified her by her crooked index finger and other details that would add to the mounting file of information being assembled.

The picture of the trunk was recognised by a dealer in second-hand luggage in the Brixton Road, who had sold the very item. The man was quite sure of his facts and said that the purchaser had said that he wanted it to store old clothes. Unfortunately the shopkeeper was not quite so clear as to the man's face and appearance.

All these investigations were models of the patience and painstaking diligence that went into the sifting of information and possible leads, and were a tribute to the force. They reflected the hard work that was put into every facet of the case. To illustrate the point, when name 'P. Holt' was investigated, it was naturally like looking for the proverbial needle in a haystack. Much time had to be spent and leg-work done to find this person; in fact she lived in Chelsea. One can never underestimate the effort that was, and still is today, applied to each item of research.

Meanwhile the jigsaw of details that would finally track down the murderer grew piece by piece. Pure coincidence also played a major part in this case. Men who knew Mrs Bonati were sought and eventually found, but nothing new in information was gleaned. However, one piece of luck came about very unexpectedly – a shoeblack had picked up a piece of crumpled paper that turned out to be the cloakroom ticket issued for the black cabin trunk. This information enabled the date to be set at 6 May, and the preceding number had been issued to a lady who had remembered the exact time that she arrived by taxi at Charing Cross. The police were then able to question taxi drivers and porters, and one of the latter remembered that the black trunk had been brought in by taxi – he recalled that it was such a tight fit in the cab that a small piece of it had broken off.

Another result of hard work and diligence was the discovery of the taxi driver involved. He said that he had driven two men to Westminster Police Court that day, and as he had set them down a man had hailed the taxi from across the road. He had asked the driver to help him into the taxi with a large black cabin trunk. The cabby was surprised at the weight of it and asked the man what was in it – 'Money?'

The man shook his head and replied, 'Books.' He was then driven to Charing Cross station.

Another useful item of information was the recollection of a bus conductor. He remembered helping a passenger to get a large black trunk aboard. The man had bought a ticket to Victoria but had alighted between Vauxhall and Victoria. The conductor could not quite remember, but it may have been Rochester Row.

The net was closing. Investigations were narrowing down the possibilities, and there was optimism in the air. Perhaps the key to the solution lay somewhere around the Rochester Row area. There is a large block of offices near where the man with the trunk had been picked up, and every person working there was interviewed, every likely query was pursued. Sure enough, a black trunk had been seen standing in one of the corridors, but bearing in mind the trust that everyone of us displays towards our fellow men, the statement that the trunk contained books had been enough to satisfy the more inquisitive minds. Several businesses in the building had gone to the wall in those troubled times, and perhaps it was the general belief that the trunk contained the effects of one of the expired firms.

The police then put in motion a search for information regarding the firms that had left the building. One of them was a firm called 'Edwards & Co, Estate & Transfer Agents'. After further enquiries it was found that the offices had been taken by a Mr John Robinson, who had started the business of Edwards & Co, in March. However, on 9 May the owner of the building received a letter from Robinson stating that he had 'gone broke' and he wished to terminate the arrangement to lease the offices. His typewriter had been repossessed, but he had paid the rent on the offices.

It was now therefore imperative to trace Mr John Robinson. Perhaps he could throw some light on the matter of the black trunk – or perhaps, as was the case with so many other people who had been interviewed. might he turn out to be yet another red herring? The cheque that he had paid to the landlord of the property led to inquiries at the bank, and it was subsequently discovered that Robinson had been living in lodgings in Camberwell, but that on 6 May he had left them, telling the landlady that he was removing to Lancashire. In fact it transpired that Robinson had taken an apartment in Kennington, and a close watch was kept on the address.

Meanwhile a telegram that Robinson had sent to a business associate had been returned to the Camberwell lodgings undelivered; in fact there had been a misunderstanding, and the person was actually at the address stated. On Thursday 19 May this person met Robinson near the Elephant & Castle. Two policemen were nearby and Robinson was invited to come to Scotland Yard for a 'chat'. At first he seemed very plausible – very helpful, in fact – and was ready with spontaneous answers to all the questions put to him. The police began to wonder if they had got the wrong man – this one seemed far from a murderer.

Robinson had done all sorts of jobs. He had been a Blackpool tram conductor, he had been in the army until he was discharged as medically unfit in 1923, he had lived in Ireland, where it was later discovered he had married bigamously, he had been a greengrocer, a bookmaker, a milkman and lots of positions as barman in a wide variety of pubs. His final throw in the world of business had been the estate agency under the name of Edwards & Co, but he had been forced to close the office due to lack of business and subsequent lack of funds. His story was that on 4 May he had met a Guardsman in a pub, and they had stayed drinking and talking until 3 pm. Then both of them had gone to Robinson's office and they had more drink until around 4.30 pm. Robinson then closed the office and went home to his lodgings. He stated, 'I have never set eyes on anybody called Mrs Bonati and I cannot remember seeing any trunk or bag in the entrance to the office on Friday 6 May'.

As luck would have it, both the man who sold the trunk and the taxi driver who took it to Charing Cross were at home ill, and they were the only people who might be expected to remember anything about the man with the black trunk. It was therefore arranged that Robinson should be paraded in front of them to see if they recognised him. They did not, as it was later discovered that he had pulled his hat down and turned the collar of his raincoat up to avoid any recognition.

The thing that impressed the police was the bare-faced cheek that Robinson showed when he met these two people. There was always the possibility that they might have remembered something about him, then his game would have been up, but he bluffed it out. So far as Robinson was concerned, he had told the police all he knew – he had been frank and open, he had answered all their questions and had nothing to hide. There was no indication that he had anything to do with black trunks or dead women, and the police let him go.

Ten days had elapsed since the discovery of the body, every line of investigation had been vigorously pursued, and nothing had turned up. After a meeting of the men involved in the case, in which the facts were thoroughly examined, it was decided that Robinson's office should be examined in minute detail. Two expert detectives were assigned to the job and an inch-by-inch search was made of the rooms.

Robinson was a heavy smoker, and the detectives found ashtrays with many cigarette ends and burnt-out matches. All the cigarette ends were studied, as were the matches – then one of the detectives came across a discoloured match; he thought that the discolouration might be blood. A dirty bloodstained duster was also found, which was in such a filthy condition that at first glance it could have contained every kind of dirt; however, when it had been cleaned there showed up some faint letters which were finally recognised as the word 'Greyhound'. It was remembered that Robinson had worked frequently as a barman, and with some effort the police found the Greyhound Hotel that had employed Robinson behind the bar and remembered him. The duster was theirs, and it was also confirmed that Robinson had bigamously married a girl who was working there.

On Monday 23 May 1927 Robinson was arrested and taken to Scotland Yard. Not much bravado now remained, and he was very keen to make a full confession. He had met Minnie Bonati at Victoria station and she had suggested that she accompany him back to his office. She had sat and waited for him as he wrote some letters, telling him that she was hard up and asked him for a pound. He had refused and she had lost her temper and become foul-mouthed. Robinson said, 'She bent down as if to pick up the poker from the fireplace. I hit her on the side of face and she fell, striking her head on the side of the fireplace. She rolled over. I left her there and went home.'

When he returned to the office the next day she was dead, and he was very surprised. 'I didn't know what to do,' he said.

He bought a knife and cut up the body, then went in search of a box large enough to put the remains in. He found a friend in a pub who helped him downstairs with the trunk, and he then called a cab and went to Charing Cross. In his panic he lost the cloakroom ticket. He buried the knife on Clapham Common, where after some trouble the police found it. (Incidentally, it had been bought at the same shop as Patrick Mahon had bought his knife and saw! – see 'The Murderous Scoundrel'.)

John Robinson was charged with murder. The prosecution experts disputed his explanation that Minnie had died from hitting her head on the fireplace surround; they found that the cause of death was probably due to a long struggle and that she had been suffocated by a cushion pressed against her mouth. This and other bruises and injuries had resulted in her painful death. The jury deliberated for an hour and a half and returned their verdict of guilty. Robinson was hanged a few days later.

40
The tale of two trunks

*B*righton – that Mecca for the tired London businessman, that Jewel of the South Coast, that glitzy, loud, brash, but 'Oh so refined' resort where Prinny's Pavilion and sundry amusement parks vie with one another for the attention of the visiting public – witnessed some most disturbing events a few years later on a sweltering hot 17 June 1934. A stinking trunk was discovered in the cloakroom on Brighton railway station. It was obviously new and made of plywood, but it stood on its own as it had been moved out of the way of other luggage due to the faint, then ever stronger, pungent smell that seemed to grow more offensive every day.

The attendants, William Vinnicombe and James Lilliott, called the police to come and investigate. Naturally no one hurried forward offering to open the trunk – presumably most of those present suspected what might be within – but they stood back and waited for a volunteer to break the lock and reveal to the world the contents. Eventually a policeman, showing more interest than the others, stepped forward, wrenched the lock off and lifted the lid.

The smell that emanated from the trunk to meet them just preceded the horrific sight of a bloody torso – minus arms, legs and feet. Several watchers left hurriedly, their hands over their mouths. A further search in the cloakroom found an old Moses basket containing the body of a few-days-old female baby, but this turned out not to be anything to do with the body in the trunk.

Detective Inspector Arthur Pelling, in charge of investigation, ordered a check of missing females in the hope of establishing the identity of the torso prior to the date the trunk was deposited, 6 June 1934. The only clue worth bothering about was a report, which was vague in the extreme, that mentioned some party guests who said they had seen a man pushing a barrow or trolley with a trunk in it or on it.

Upon investigation Sir Bernard Spilsbury, the eminent pathologist, was certain that the torso was that of a 5 ft 2 in female weighing between 8 and 9 stone and aged from 21 to 28 years, well nourished, pregnant and probably coming from a middle-class background.

Meanwhile at King's Cross left luggage office a few weeks later a porter named William Cope thought he was aware of a smell coming from a cheap fibre suitcase. Upon opening it he was horrified to find two legs and two feet wrapped in newspapers soaked in olive oil. The police's immediate thoughts were that they might match the torso found in Brighton.

When the news of the discovery of the legs and feet broke, a certain Mr Tony Mancini was very interested. He lived in Brighton and went under several aliases, of which Mancini was one. He was an expert dancer, but was usually employed as a waiter. Latterly a prostitute's pimp, he lived with one Violette Kaye, married but parted from a John Saunders. Tony looked after her affairs, but they used to have violent quarrels, although they would eventually kiss and make up.

However, one night they had a dreadful row in which Tony lost his temper. He picked up a coal hammer and threw it at Violette – it struck her on the head with such force that it killed her. Tony did not know what to do with the body, so he put it in the wardrobe in its state of rigor mortis. When this wore off and the body began to sag and make strange noises, he went out and bought a black fibre trunk and stuffed the body in it. He decided that he would have to move, and found a dingy run-down house in Kemp Street where he could settle down. Two of his mates helped him to move – they remarked on the weight of the trunk, but Tony laughed it off.

For a time Tony used the trunk as a seat with a floral cloth draped over it, then it inevitably began to smell and leak – it would have to go. However, Tony decided to live with it for the time being as he had to be very wary of where the trunk and its stinking contents went.

Meanwhile the local police took over several rooms at the Brighton Pavilion to use as a base for their inquiries into the case of the other trunk and its grim contents. Rumour was rife in Brighton and the town was full of speculation. A clairvoyant was called in, perhaps to give a lead as to who the murderer might be; he came up with the prediction that the man the police should look for was probably called George, had bushy hair, worked for a seed merchant and had obtained the brown paper in which the torso was wrapped from a tyre dealer. The police had been inundated with reports of sightings of men pushing strange-looking boxes. These men had all looked sinister, but most of the reports were spurious. All the same they had to be checked and counter-checked for their veracity.

Then a breakthrough occurred that was to lead to the apprehension of a suspect. A man, possibly an old client, called at the address where Tony had killed Violette before moving to Kemp Street. The man wanted to see Violette for business reasons, and the landlady told him that Mr and Mrs Mancini had gone. Eventually the police found Mancini washing up in the Skylark Cafe. He told them that Violette had gone to ply her trade in France and Germany; he also told the police that she was 42 years old.

Tony, full of thoughts about the terrible contents of the trunk, decided nonetheless to enjoy the company of a young girl that he had met recently. He took her to the Aqua Cafe for fish and chips, but he was morose and not his cheerful self, The girl noticed a difference in him, and halfway through his meal he stood up, made his apologies and left. He hurried home, packed a few things into a suitcase and got on the train for London to lie low until the situation cooled down.

As a result of their enquiries in and around the seamier areas of Brighton, the local police were told of Mancini's Kemp Street address. Seeking to pursue their enquiries further they arrived at the house and banged on the door. The house was empty, although the exterior was festooned with scaffolding as the decorators were busy while the owner was away on holiday. The police needed to gain access to follow up their hunch that something inside would solve a long-standing crime, so they broke down the door. The smell led them upstairs, and in a back bedroom they found the trunk, by this time reeking and standing in a pool of evil-smelling liquid. On breaking the lock they found the rapidly decomposing body of Violette Kaye.

Mancini was arrested in London a few days later. At his trial at Lewes Assizes, he was defended by the eminent barrister Norman Birkett KC, a very clever advocate who managed to turn Mancini's lies into believable rhetoric. The jury, in their deliberations, believed Mancini's lies and he was acquitted.

By coincidence a gangland mobster who had disposed of a rival villain and suffered the ultimate hanging was also called Tony Mancini!

Meanwhile Brighton trunk murder No 1 was still causing the police many headaches. In spite of exhaustive investigations and thousands of interviews, nothing had been found. Chief Inspector Donaldson, who was now in charge of the case, was, however, a dogged, stubborn man, and he stuck to the case believing that one day someone's cover might slip and suspicions might bear fruit. A meeting was held involving the local constabulary at all levels try to bring the case to a conclusion.

All the evidence was examined and analysed in great detail, and a planned covert observation of the comings and goings of a certain doctor, who had a private practice in Hove and was rumoured to specialise in illegal abortions, was mounted. However, the representative of the Hove police who was at the meeting decided to take things into his own hands; he went to see the doctor and bluntly told him of the suspicions held by the police. As this policeman was reminding him of the seriousness of the case, the good doctor was making copious notes. Eventually the doctor rose from the table and handed the officer a list of prominent residents who lived in the Brighton and Hove area who had the reputation of being public benefactors and had great influence. The doctor then told the officer that if he did not call off the investigations he would use these powerful people to 'speak' to the higher authorities in the police force to deal with anyone who attempted to sully his name. The policeman saw his own way out – he had heard enough.

Chief Inspector Donaldson was furious. Because of the police officer's action, the big fish had wriggled off the hook. Possibly the doctor had taken fright after all, because not long afterwards he moved to London where he again set up in practice. However, a young girl died after receiving his dubious attentions shortly afterwards, and a few years later he left England, and was subsequently struck off the Medical Register. The murder, however, remained on the police books, and no one was ever convicted.

41
The murderous scoundrel

*M*isuse of a railway cloakroom also figures in the closing moments of this gruesome story. Patrick Herbert Mahon was a charming, suave, handsome and personable example of the human race. He was also a murderer, a liar, a cheat, a thief, an embezzler and he possessed a cool, calculating mind that got him out of many troublesome tight corners. Born in Liverpool, one of a large family of middle-class stock, he showed some talent at school and became very devoted to the local Sunday School. When he left school he managed to find a job as an office boy, and eventually a junior clerk. He still went to church and took a great interest in the social activities connected with it; in other words, he was the perfect model of a good, clean-living young man.

At school he had met a pretty, dark-haired girl with whom he was to have a strange but tumultuous relationship. She would always understand him, know him and be able to read him like a book, and he would return to her and pour out his heart in the many times that he was in serious trouble, and those occasions were many. In the early days they were very much in love and were in their teens when he first asked Ann to marry him. Both families opposed such a union, but two years later, in 1910, they got married; Pat was 20 and Ann 18. It was a daring marriage, but if anyone could succeed in keeping Pat on the straight and narrow it was Ann – when she got the chance! She was singularly devoted to him to the very end and his weaknesses were her strengths.

His capacity to defraud and swindle did not take long to develop. They had only been married a year when he forged a cheque for £123 on the company who employed him; he fled but was caught in the Isle of Man where he had taken a young girl he had picked up for a few day's holiday. He was lucky – the court slapped his wrists and bound him over. Ann forgave him and they left Liverpool to start a new life.

He managed to get a job with a dairy company in Wiltshire – he had undoubted business ability and he got on well with his fellow men. He was very fond of soccer and played for a local team. At around this time a daughter arrived, but at the same time he was arrested for embezzling £60 from his employers. This time the Judge at Dorchester Assizes sentenced him to 12 months imprisonment.

On his release he is known to have lived in the Calne area, and while he was in the district there was a sudden spate of burglaries – a coincidence, possibly? Whatever, suddenly the Mahons decided to move on again. This time Sunningdale became their home, and he was again taken on by a dairy (dairies seem to have figured much in Mahon's working life – perhaps it is because he displayed a marked propensity for milking people. . .). At Sunningdale he had some minor love affairs with the local lasses, nothing spectacular, then was again out of work. He had shown great interest in horse racing, and the next we hear of him he had become a turf accountant's clerk.

One night in the early months of 1916 a branch of the National Provincial Bank was broken into. The intruder was disturbed by a servant girl who was savagely beaten with a hammer, rendering her unconscious, but when she came to she found herself in Mahon's arms and he was kissing her! He fled to Wallasey, but was traced and brought back to be tried at Guildford Assizes. In spite of his pathetic appeal that he wanted to join the army, the presiding Judge thought otherwise and sentenced him to five years penal servitude.

A son was born to Ann in 1916, but he died 18 months later without ever seeing his father. Ann, meanwhile, had made a new life on her own. She had found a job with Console Aerators in Sudbury; she was good at her jobs and her diligence and efficiency moved her up the firm's promotional ladder to a position of trust and respect. When Mahon came out of prison full of promises and good intentions he was pleased to see his wife and daughter – he would never stray from the law again, and that was a promise, on his life!

Ann took him back as she always did. But it did not stop him ogling other girls that attracted his practised eye – he was always willing to take any young woman out! The Mahons moved to London and lived in a flat in Kew. Ann found Pat a job as a traveller with Console Aerators, and he did well, selling a lot of products. The firm was pleased with his progress, but something had gone badly wrong and in May 1922 the Receivers were called in; they continued to operate the company and appointed Patrick Mahon Sales Manager.

It so happened that the Receivers also appointed a typist called Miss Emily Bealby Kaye, and she was to meet an untimely, horrific end at the hands of Patrick Mahon. Miss Kaye was a self- sufficient, capable person who could look after herself in more ways than one; she managed her financial affairs very well and did not object to an affair with the handsome, personable Sales Manager. The affair gathered pace; she fell in love with Pat, but he treated it as just another episode, and certainly did not want it to get serious and out of hand. Just before Christmas Miss Kaye was dismissed by the Receivers, and wanted to see more of Pat; he was not too bothered, but felt sorry for her as she was now out of work. He began to appear more frequently at her house, but felt a bit embarrassed at her strong feelings for him, and wanted to keep her at arm's length.

Emily managed to obtain another job, but it did not last long and she was out of work gain. In February 1924 she realised that she was pregnant. Mahon said that she wanted him to go abroad with her, but he did not want to go and told her so; he did agree to consider the proposal and suggested that they should take a bungalow by the seaside for a week or two. Emily was not so easily deterred – she wanted Mahon and she was not going to let him go. This was to be her undoing.

At that time Mahon was for once not worried by financial constraints; he was happy at his work and was popular among his friends. He became secretary of the local bowling club and his future looked bright – apart from his long-suffering wife no one knew of his shady past, but if he gave in to Emily all that he had achieved would slide away. But fate decided to take a hand: Emily was clearing out a drawer and at the bottom she found a sheet of newspaper. She could not recall having seen it before, but there it was – the sordid history of Patrick Mahon's trial at Guildford Assizes.

Emily decided to use this new information to pressurise Pat into doing her bidding – in other words blackmail. Perhaps it was this change of attitude on Emily's part that decided Pat to kill her. He arranged to lease a former Coast Guard bungalow on a remote stretch of beach between Eastbourne and Pevensey for two months, using the name of Waller. Emily sold her stocks and shareholdings and went down to Eastbourne to look over the place; Mahon arranged to join her later.

He did not like what he felt he had to do, but now Emily had her hooks well and truly into him, and her demands were getting on his nerves. Two days before he was due to go to join her at the bungalow, he met a total stranger, a Miss Duncan, in the street. On a cold wet night he escorted her home to Richmond, told her that his life was a tragedy and asked her to have dinner with him on the following Wednesday. He must have had plans to dispose of Emily by this time, yet he was inviting a stranger to have dinner with him!

The next day he bought a saw and a knife at a shop in Victoria Street and journeyed down to Eastbourne. Emily was at the station to meet him. (Incidentally, Mahon was supposed to be travelling on business and not setting up home with a lady in Eastbourne.) Emily had set her heart on living in South Africa, and she wanted Mahon to elope with her. She had already told her friends that she had got engaged, and in a letter written to a friend on 14 April she said that she and 'Pat' were going to Paris for a few days before setting out for South Africa.

She now tried to put pressure on Mahon to apply for a passport, but he was having none of this pressure. Tempers became frayed and in her fury she threw an axe at him, then attacked him with her bare hands. In his version of what happened next, they fell and she struck her head on a brass coal scuttle; after a minute or two he realised that she was dead.

He left the bungalow and returned home to Ann. She was not surprised to see him – she was used to his comings and goings. On the Wednesday he wined and dined Miss Duncan, mentioning casually that he had a 'place' at Eastbourne and would she like to come down and see the sea? She agreed to come two days later. No one other than a lunatic would have chanced his arm like Mahon – he now had to get rid of Emily's body pretty quickly. When Miss Duncan arrived at the bungalow he showed her round, apart from one room – 'It contains valuable books,' he explained. The next day he took her to Plumpton Races, where he ran into an old friend and put on a good act to cover up his shaken mental state.

As soon as he could, Mahon went back to the bungalow – he had work to do. He partly dismembered Emily's body and decided to burn the remains. He built a large fire and put the head on the red-hot coals. At that moment the storm that had been threatening all afternoon broke with a terrific crash of thunder, as the head lay on the fiery ashes the eyes opened and Mahon, by this time in a state of shock as he realised what he was doing, fled from the building and ran along the rainy, windswept beach.

When he had plucked up sufficient courage to return, the fire had done its work. However, he had to get rid of the remaining parts of the body, so he cut them up and packed the bits into a Gladstone bag and decided to dispose of them by throwing them out of a railway carriage window. He did get rid of some of the pieces between Waterloo and Richmond, but not enough, so he tried again the next night – daytime was too risky. Eventually he was left with the empty bag, some of the wrappings he had used to contain the gruesome contents and the razor-sharp knife that he had used. He decided to leave the bag in one of the cloakrooms at Waterloo station and went home to Ann.

She did not know what was going on – how could she? But she found the cloakroom ticket and told a friend who had some connection with the railway police, asking him to investigate. When he took possession of the bag it was locked, and as it was forced open the smell was awful – but the evidence was there. Scotland Yard was informed, and Chief Inspector Savage posted men to keep an eye on the cloakroom.

Mahon turned up for the bag on the Friday evening, was arrested and taken to Scotland Yard. The bag's contents revealed the sharp knife, two pieces of silk, a towel, a silk scarf, a pair of torn lady's knickers and a brown canvas racket case – all the items were spattered with blood. A thorough search was made of the bungalow at Eastbourne, and more human remains were discovered; evidence was found of the gruesome attempts to butcher the torso, but no sign of the head remained, so the exact cause of death was never discovered.

Mahon's trial opened at Lewes Assizes in July 1924 and Mahon was found guilty and sentenced to be hanged. Thus ended this barbaric litany of gruesome events. The sheer audacity of Mahon's work was shocking in the extreme, and the public could permit themselves a sigh of relief at his execution.

42
Caught by telegraph

'Crimes of passion', and indeed cold-blooded murders, committed by lovers are of course very much older than the railways, but soon began to figure in the annals of railway crime.

In the 1840s the railways of Britain were still in the process of invention. Safety had become important, improvements in communication were just beginning to be discovered, and the passenger had become a valued customer to be attracted to rail travel.

The Great Western Railway was often the first with new innovations, and in 1843 the company conducted an experimental exercise in telegraphic communication between Slough and Paddington, consisting of two heavy-duty wires on poles situated by the side of the track. The system worked and another milestone in railway history had been achieved. The system was adopted by the GWR and the electromagnetic telegraph, invented by Professor Wheatstone and Mr W. F. Cooke, was acclaimed by the grateful company.

John Tawell was a convict. Sentenced to 21 years for forgery, he was sent to a prison colony in Botany Bay, but was fortunate enough to obtain a 'ticket of leave' and was able to return to England. He decided to strike the pose of a Quaker, no doubt thinking of getting into pure society and looking round for any opportunity to make money without a great deal of effort.

He adopted the dress of the Quakers and became part of their number, attending their services and professing to espouse their cause. He was also able to make the acquaintance of a wealthy Quaker widow who was attracted by his looks and charm. He would visit her in her large house and be waited on by her servants. Things soon became serious, and although the lady's family did not think much of him and his charm, Tawell subsequently married the lady.

He then led the life of Riley. Money was no object. His wife did as she was told and handed over large sums of money on request. Nothing was out of his reach. He cultivated her rich friends, joined the appropriate clubs and wormed his way into the local society. It was noted that he 'seemed a decent generous fellow'. His activities among the religious members of the local society were appreciated – he gave generously and professed to have many contacts.

Beneath the surface, however, Tawell was becoming bored. His wife found him wanting more and more money. She was not getting satisfactory answers to her questions about his past. She also noticed how well he was able to draw and sketch. She even found him copying her signature one day. He laughed the matter off, but suspicions were beginning to form in her mind.

Tawell was looking around for more excitement. He was now finding his wife stale and unattractive. Her money was very useful but she now seemed very suspicious and kept questioning him about his past, which annoyed and frightened him. He certainly did not want her to find out that he was a convicted forger.

One day he met a very comely young lady named Sarah Hart who lived in a cottage at Salt Hill near Slough. At first she suited his desires and he managed to see a good deal of her without disturbing his lifestyle with Mrs Tawell. Tawell confided in Sarah much of his background, mainly when in the frequent passionate embraces that excited him so much. He soon realised, however, that he was talking too much, and when finally their relationship too became stale and meaningless, he found that he could soon find himself in a very compromising situation.

He spent many sleepless nights racked by worries about what he could do to rid himself of the memories of his lawless past. His wife was distant from him now. She kept looking at him with suspicion and he could feel her eyes drilling into him, looking for reasons that would satisfy her doubts.

Then he made up his mind. Sarah Hart would have to be bought off or silenced for good. Having the opportunity to call on her to wish her well for the New Year of 1845, Tawell went to Salt Hill to offer his good wishes; indeed, his last wishes, because in his pocket was enough cyanide to kill ten men.

He tried to reason with her. He wanted his freedom, the friendship was over. But she wouldn't let him go. No money would satisfy her, she only wanted him. She then began to suggest ways and means by which she could keep him for herself. In other words, she would spill the beans about his past to 'certain people' whom she was sure would be very interested. Tawell knew now that she had to be killed.

In an attempt to smooth things over Tawell suggested that they should share a bottle of stout. Sarah agreed and poured out two glasses.

When she left the room Tawell tipped a hefty dose of the cyanide into her glass and watched her face become contorted with agony as the poison began to destroy her body. She began to scream out in pain, and Tawell fled as the neighbours heard the cries and came to investigate.

He made for the station at Slough. Unfortunately for him, one of the neighbours had seen him leave the cottage and had told the local vicar. The alarm was raised. The vicar was given a description of Tawell and as he reached the station he saw the man he believed to be Tawell climb aboard the 7.42 pm train for Paddington.

Mr Howell, the Station Master at Slough, after talking to the vicar, decided to use the newfangled telegraph system based at Telegraph Cottage near the station in an attempt to get the news of the fugitive to Paddington before the train arrived at its destination.

The message was: 'A murder has just been committed at Salt Hill and the suspect has been seen to take a first class ticket to Paddington on the 7.42 pm. He is dressed as a Quaker with a long overcoat down to his ankles. He is sitting in the second first class carriage.'

The message was received at Paddington with delight and the staff there sent a reply to Slough as follows: 'The up train has arrived and a person answering your description sent by telegraph has been seen getting out of the carriage. He was seen boarding an omnibus in New Road and our Sergeant Williams is following him.'

The resourceful Sergeant Williams put an overcoat over his uniform and was able to see Tawell leaving the train. Williams followed his quarry on to the omnibus and assumed the role of conductor. Tawell left the bus at the corner of Princes Street and, as the respectable Quaker he purported to be, he handed his ticket to Williams!

Williams also left the bus and discreetly followed the suspect. Tawell walked at a leisurely pace to Cornhill. The Sergeant was in sight of him but drew no attention. Tawell entered the Jerusalem Coffee House, and after a while emerged and walked to a public house called the Leopard. He had one or two drinks there, then walked to a lodging house in Scott's Yard near Cannon Street.

Sergeant Williams waited patiently for over an hour, then returned to his base at Paddington. He might have lost Tawell, but he had to consult his superiors about what to do next. Luckily for the railway police Tawell was a creature of habit and the following morning, when Williams, now in uniform, walked into the Jerusalem Coffee House, who should be there sipping coffee but Tawell!

He was visibly shaken when Sergeant Williams told him to accompany him to Slough to the house of a woman found dead! His composure returned, however, and he kept his head as he replied, 'My integrity in life will be upheld by my station in society.'

He could not have been more wrong, as he found out at his trial at Aylesbury Assizes. In spite of a spirited defence, the jury found him guilty of murder, and the judge reached for the black cap. Tawell had made history as the first man to be caught by the use of the electric telegraph. He was hanged for his crime. History had been made and justice had been seen to be satisfied.

43
The Ballybrophy murder

*W*hen the Great Southern & Western Railway of Ireland was spreading its empire in the first half of the 19th century, men to build the track, bridges, culverts, cuttings, tunnels and every aspect of the railway were brought in for their fitness and sheer muscle power – how they could dig and lift and graft for weeks on end. Rest camps were tough, primitive places where men whose morals were often of a dubious character, would live side by side, often with explosive results.

Such was the case with the GS&WR. The station at Ballybrophy was completed in September 1847, and two months later a murder was committed. The permanent way was looked after by gangers, platelayers and lengthmen who patrolled stretches of the track, re-packing ballast and checking joints and sleepers as part of the ongoing maintenance of the line. In those far-off days the type of man who would undertake that sort of work was usually a labourer who had joined the permanent way gang between other jobs. They did not have to be of high intellect or possess skills other than reliability, a broad back and good eyesight.

Jon D'Arcy was a labourer with a GS&WR PW gang. However, he was unreliable, slow, lazy and troublesome in the way that he would try to stir up trouble among the others in the gang. His conduct left a lot to be desired, and he had been warned about his work and general behaviour, but he took no notice. In the end he was sacked. D'Arcy was a vengeful man and he bore terrible grudges, and for his dismissal from the PW gang he blamed Michael Smith, the ganger, and he swore that he would get even.

He did not go far away from Ballybrophy station, but hung about planning to kill Smith. One day James Carey, a lamp-cleaner on the GS&WR, met D'Arcy on the railway track. D'Arcy had hidden between some carriages and jumped out on Carey.

'You're not the man I want!' he said, then Smith ran up and said 'I'm the man you want, and if you don't keep out of my way, I will let the light through you and swear my life against you in the morning!'

D'Arcy and one John Coonan remained hidden amongst the railway coaches. When Smith came out of the enginemen's shed he asked a man called Michael Fahy to come over to the siding in which the carriages were stabled, saying that he wanted to speak to someone over there.

Fahy said, 'Go to the Devil!', then shoved him out of the shed and slammed the door on him. John Coonan leapt at Smith and hit him on the side of the head with a stone, knocking him down; Smith hit his head on the rail, D'Arcy then came forward and started raining large stones on Smith's head; Coonan then hit him with a thick stick that broke across him. Smith never cried out or stirred – he gave just one big sigh. The men then ran off towards Templemore.

John Bailey found Smith's body, having heard the sounds of the shouting and the scuffles. Patrick Gorman, a 'tent-keeper', reported that he had seen D'Arcy between 7 and 8 o'clock on the night of the murder within about a dozen yards of the engine shed where Smith was killed.

D'Arcy meanwhile had made his way to Cork and got a job in a PW gang working near Kilbarry. However, he was dismissed again for stirring up trouble and general misconduct, and again he threatened the ganger who had sacked him with murder. He then joined the Army, got hopelessly drunk, started boasting about his triumph in murdering Ganger Smith and was duly arrested.

Private Sarsfield of the 67th Regiment said that the prisoner D'Arcy had boasted to him that he had killed a man named Smith, a ganger on the GS&WR Borris-in-Ossory and Ballybrophy. Gerald Burns, a railway ganger, had met D'Arcy in Cork where he had been working under a ganger named Johnson; D'Arcy had been heard by Burns to say that 'He would have revenge and clip him as he had clipped the ganger Smith. Burns had written to Mr Thacker, a magistrate at Borris-in-Ossory, to have D'Arcy arrested for murder.

D'Arcy's trial took place in Maryborough on Wednesday and Thursday 15-16 March 1848, and was reported in the *Drogheda Conservative Journal* of 18 March. Judge Doherty was presiding and D'Arcy was accused that he 'on the night of the 13th day of November, by force of arms, at Ballybrophy, in the King's County, feloniously, maliciously and with malice prepense did kill and murder one Michael Smith, striking him on the head, which inflicted a wound three inches long and two inches deep, of which he did instantly die, and that John Coonan aided and abetted John D'Arcy so to do. . .' There were other accounts of the description of the murder alleged to have been committed with a shovel or a big stick.

Mr J. Adye Curran was in the act of cross-examining D'Arcy when the Judge intervened to say that 'he considered D'Arcy to be one of the most consummate scoundrels he had come across in 40 years practice'. The jury, after taking much time in their deliberations, returned a verdict of guilty. His Lordship informed the prisoner that he would not sentence him that evening, but told him that 'his time in the World would be very brief'. The prisoner then became outrageous, and knocked his hat against the ground shouting that he was innocent of the murder, notwithstanding all that had been sworn against him by informers. After this painful scene the Court adjourned.

On the following day, 'His Lordship now addressed the unhappy culprit, who threw himself on to his knees and begged for a long day . . . the Judge pronounced sentence of Death by Hanging, D'Arcy received the sentence, still in the kneeling position, but did not demean himself in the reckless manner which had marked his conduct on the previous evening.' After the sentence he had to be supported by two turnkeys and removed from the Court. John D'Arcy was hanged on the lawn in front of Maryborough Jail. It was market day, but the crowd of approximately 300 had seen other public executions before and this was not particularly interesting or different.

D'Arcy was undoubtedly a violent man, and in the eyes of his fellows richly deserved his sentence of death. His case reminds us all of the social conditions and rigours of life in those days when the coming of the railway brought with it the problems of men working together under adverse conditions. It is a pity that the life of Michael Smith should have been taken under those circumstances.

44
Murder on the Limerick goods

One would naturally assume that, in most cases, the relationship between the driver and fireman on a steam locomotive is essentially good. At least, that is what the general public hope is the case, for if the reverse is true, the risk of disagreements and potential violence in the limited amount of space on the footplate of any steam loco could mean trouble, both for the smooth running of the train and the safety of the passengers.

This question of relationships no doubt did not often cross the passenger's thoughts. They saw the driver and fireman on the footplate and they assumed that this established team would take them smoothly to their destination; the very idea of the driver and fireman not actually getting on together with its attendant problems belonged to the silver screen or the more sensational newspapers. However, despite every care taken by the railway company to make sure that the driver and fireman worked well together, such an ideal situation was not always possible, and fights and violent arguments were known to occur from time to time.

Staying in Ireland, we have a story about one such relationship, which got completely out of hand with tragic results. The location of this turbulent tale is the little town of Buttevant, north of Mallow in the County of Limerick in what is now the Republic of Ireland. The year is 1873, the month is April and the evening goods train from Limerick to Cork is being hauled, not by the regular locomotive, which had failed the previous night, but by No 123, which was an 0-4-2 tender engine built at Inchicore Works in the 1860s.

The driver was Arnold Wall, known to his many friends as 'Archy', and the fireman was Timothy Nagle. As was the custom, the train had two brake-vans, one at the rear of the train and the other coupled behind the engine. In the front brake-van was Head Guard Thomas

Wiseman, and in the rear vehicle was Michael Donovan. The scheduled starting time from Limerick was 6.25 pm, but the train was running late on that particular evening and did not leave Limerick until 6.55 pm; time would have to be made up somewhere.

It was not until Charleville was reached at 9.35 pm that it was realised that the timing was still down 30 minutes on schedule. The shunting complete, the train moved out of Charleville station towards its next stop at Buttevant, but about 2 miles down the line the train began to slow down and eventually stopped. Wiseman, who was near the engine, called out to the footplate crew to ask what was wrong, but there was no reply, so he got out of the brake-van and walked up to the locomotive.

The footplate was deserted. Wall and Nagle had disappeared. Donovan joined him and they used the far from adequate light from their lamps to search the immediate area. Wiseman told Donovan to go back down the line and fix warning detonators to protect the train according to the company's Rules and Regulations. The two guards then went back together, and some 40 yards from the rear of the train they found a cap lying beside the line. They reasoned that by some strange accident the two men had fallen from the loco.

The goods train was standing motionless on the busy main line, so Wiseman decided to walk forward to Buttevant station to report the incident and obtain further instructions. He started to walk along the 'four-foot', as the area between the rails is known to railwaymen, shining his lamp and looking for signs of the two men, but with no success. He walked into Buttevant station and informed Station Master Cashell of what had happened. Mr Cashell was concerned at the news and decided to go back with Wiseman to find Donovan and resume the search. In the meantime the northbound 'Night Mail' had stopped in Buttevant station awaiting instructions to proceed; Mr Cashell informed the crew of the situation, and directed the driver to go forward at a very slow speed while he and Wiseman walked ahead towards the goods train.

After Wiseman had left for Buttevant, Donovan had resumed his search, and about 20 yards from where the cap had been discovered he came across Wall, his face contorted in a congealed mask of blood. He was dead, and one of his arms was draped across the rail. Donovan placed a stone under Wall's head and went back to the train to await Wiseman's return.

Upon arrival, Station Master Cashell examined Wall first and agreed that he was beyond help. Now he had to decide how to clear the line for the southbound 'Night Mail' from Dublin, due to leave Limerick Junction at 12.10 am. It would soon be bearing down on them, so he instructed John Quirk, the fireman of the northbound train, to examine No 123. Quirk did so and found the engine with a good fire, the water in the boiler satisfactory and the fire door ajar; however, the tender brake had not been applied, and there was no sign of the fireman's shovel or coal-pick, although the other tools seemed to be in place. He declared the engine fit to proceed, so Cashell ordered him to drive the train on to Mallow; Wiseman was to go with him to act as guard and fireman.

The goods train duly set off and made a halt at Buttevant, where Quirk had a good look round the engine. In the firebox he found the remains of the shovel, the wooden handle burnt away and even the blade distorted with the extreme heat. More importantly he found that the tender footsteps had blood on them, and there were more signs of blood on the handrails and the brass edging of the firebox top. Resuming the journey, the goods train eventually reached Mallow where Quirk ran the engine into the loco yard and told the steam-raiser, Edmund McDonnell, to keep an eye on her until the police arrived. At this point Quirk noticed that the heavy hammer that all locos carried was in the toolbox. There were three cleaners at work at the shed, and Quirk warned McDonnell not to move the engine. However, a strange thing happened, and about an hour later, when McDonnell came back to look over the engine, the heavy hammer had disappeared.

The discovery of Archy Wall's body had not solved the disappearance of Timothy Nagle. Was he too lying injured and bleeding by the trackside? Cashell did not know, and the situation was worrying. Midnight was approaching and the northbound 'Mail' could not be left waiting much longer, so Cashell ordered the driver to proceed very slowly with Donovan and himself walking ahead swinging their lamps in order to keep a look out for Nagle. As they approached the level crossing at Shinanagh the crossing-keeper, Peter Heleghan, came out of his cottage to greet them. Cashell told him of the tragedy and the search for Nagle, to which Heleghan replied that Nagle was alive and well and was in the cottage.

Heleghan explained that at about 11.30 he had looked out of the cottage and saw a stranger at the crossing gates wearing only a shirt and vest. He had called out, 'What's the matter with you?', and the stranger had asked him if he could come into the cottage and stay the night, and could he lend him some clothes?

Nagle then told Heleghan the long story of how he had arrived at Shinanagh. He said that he was on the engine with Archy Wall and wanted to put coal in the fire, but Wall would not let him open the firebox door. Nagle then made as if to hit Wall and the two men 'jostled'. Nagle said that Wall had trapped his (Nagle's) hand in the door, there was more 'jostling' and Wall fell off the engine. Nagle was frightened and jumped off the footplate on to what he thought was grass, but it was a bog, or so Nagle claimed, and he became so soaked that he peeled his clothes off, even his boots and stockings, and threw them away.

Heleghan took in the story, lent Nagle clothes and said he could stay the night. He asked Nagle where he thought the train was. Nagle said it had been moved to Buttevant – as regards Wall, he said, 'I might as well be dead, the way he was with me.'

Nagle then asked Heleghan not to tell anyone he was at Shinanagh, but Heleghan was taking no chances; he was not sure that he believed Nagle's story, but he had no proof one way or the other.

When Heleghan told Cashell that Nagle was in the cottage, the Station Master went in to talk to him. Nagle seemed very disturbed and talked excitedly about Wall and how they disliked one another; Cashell warned him not to say too much for fear of incriminating himself. The 'Mail' was allowed to resume its journey, as there seemed no reason to hold it up any longer.

About half an hour later a goods train came through and was stopped. The body of Archy Wall was lifted into a wagon, and Cashell took Nagle with him on the loco to Charleville. On arrival Nagle was detained in a waiting room and one of the company's policemen, John Ryan, was sent for. Nagle was asleep when Ryan arrived, but on waking he answered the questions Ryan put to him freely. His story was again that Wall had closed the firehole door on his hand and the shovel had slipped into the fire, hard words were exchanged and then some 'jostling' had taken place, after which Wall had fallen on to the track. He had jumped off into a bog, had peeled off his clothes, which would seem downright impossible to do in those circumstances, had managed at last to get out, had seen a light and staggered towards it, finding Shinanagh and Peter Heleghan.

Ryan examined Nagle's hand – there was a slight mark or scratch but nothing to suggest a first-degree burn which would have been the case if one had had a hand trapped in a firebox door, so this part of Nagle's story was no longer quite convincing. Indeed, those who knew of the bad relationship between Nagle and Wall smiled at his explanation; these two hated one another and this fact was very well known. Cashell, too, doubted the story that Nagle had put forward as a true record of events.

Nagle was removed to the local constabulary barracks under arrest and was brought to Mallow for the inquest on Archy Wall the following day. The inquest was told of the bad feeling between the two men, how they had worked together for about six months and were seen to be quarrelling on many occasions. Once Nagle had forced open Wall's toolbox, and Wall had complained to Station Master Jack O'Leary at Mallow about his fireman's aggressive attitude; O'Leary's advice was 'Throw him off the engine if he doesn't behave, Archy'. Misconduct on the footplate of an engine was regarded as very serious by the railway company, and if proved it usually resulted in dismissal.

The Head porter at Mallow, Hugh McMahon, told of how Wall was shunting some wagons one day and the engine was delayed in the exercise. It was found that Wall and Nagle were having a serious row as to whether the fire needed more coal – Nagle was seen to strike Wall on his legs with the shovel and Wall gave in and let Nagle throw on more coal. McMahon spoke to Nagle, telling him to have more respect for Wall as he was his senior on the footplate.

On the very evening of the tragedy, a shunter at Charleville had overheard arguing going on between the two men. He had heard Wall saying to Nagle, 'You talk too much', but none of the witnesses seemed to think the bad will was too serious, as they always seemed to be friendly after a quarrel.

The police searched the bog into which Nagle had tumbled that fateful night, and they found the clothing as he had described; it consisted of 'a working coat made of canvas, a black cloth coat, black corduroy trousers, flannel under pants'. He had wrapped a woollen scarf round his neck to keep himself warm on his walk to Shinanagh, together with his soaking vest and shirt. These garments were examined by Professor J. Emerson Reynolds in Dublin, who stated that he had found blood on the coat, but that the clothes were well soaked in the bog waters and inevitably any bloodstains might have been dissipated. The coat, however, had been folded and had not lost the bloodstains, a very strange situation indeed.

The body of the dead driver Archy Wall was examined by Dr Parsons Berry of Mallow, who reported that he had found 'a cut under the left eye about an inch long, in connection with the fracture of the cheek bone underneath, the nose was fractured, there was a contusion on the right temple in a downward direction, there were several contusions on the back of the head and neck, there was an extravasation of blood under the scalp corresponding with each of these contusions and a considerable amount of blood effused on the surface and at the base of the brain.'

With this information it was possible to recreate the fateful event. It seemed that Nagle's temper had boiled over, sick of old Wall and his unreasonable ways, and that they had been rowing as usual over trivial matters. Wall had said something tactless and Nagle had overreacted – he had the shovel in his hands and he had hit Wall a terrible blow that had smashed his cheek bone and ripped open his face. His head had crashed back against the boiler mountings so that he severely injured the back of his head and neck, blood had spurted out of the wound in his head, he had fallen down in a heap on the footplate, and Nagle had heaved him out on to the track. Nagle had then shut off the steam, but in his panic had not applied the brakes. He had then realised that his clothing was covered in Wall's blood, so he had begun to strip off and had soaked the clothes in a nearby bog to remove the bloodstains; he had nearly removed all the evidence except for the coat, which had folded as he pushed it into the bog and the bloodstains had remained in the material.

His alternative story was weak in the extreme, and surely he realised that it would not stand up in a Court of Law – how many people would believe that Archy Wall had died from a fall from the engine footplate? No, the driver had bled to death from the injuries sustained by Nagle's attack. The Coroner's jury found that Archy Wall had been killed by Timothy Nagle, and the latter's next move was to Cork Jail to await his trial for murder.

At the Summer Assizes of 1873, held in the Court House of Cork City, Timothy Nagle went on trial for his life. The Judge was Michael Morris (later to be created Lord Killanin), and the Court opened on the morning of 23 July. The case for the Crown was led by Sergeant Sir Colman O'Loghlen, James Sullivan Green QC, and Henry O'Hea BA. Representing Nagle against this formidable legal firepower was Peter O'Brien BA, a young man of about 23 years but possessor of much confidence. A model of locomotive No 123 was in the courtroom on display to perhaps illustrate the scene of the crime as it might be reconstructed by either side.

As it happened, the trial lasted for one day only; an attempt was made by the defence to avoid the disclosure of the bad relationship between Wall and Nagle, but without success. Nagle's advocate called no witnesses; it would have been no good, since most people were well aware of the bad blood that had existed between the two men. Mr O'Brien tried to prove that the rage that had incited Nagle to attack Wall was 'on the spur of the moment', and that the attack was not planned, so the charge of murder should be changed to manslaughter. The Judge agreed and told the jury that 'although the charge had been named as Murder, yet the crime had been certainly no more than Manslaughter'. These remarks certainly gave the man in the dock cause for a sigh of relief.

'But,' said the Judge, 'the killing of Archy Wall was unlawful and there was no evidence that anyone but he and Nagle had been on the footplate of engine No 123 that night.'

In short, the Judge directed the jury to find the verdict that they agreed on after deliberations. Two days later Nagle again stood before Judge Morris and heard him say that he would be sentenced to 20 years' imprisonment for the manslaughter of Archy Wall. In fact he served 15 years of penal servitude for his crime, and after studying the available evidence I feel that he was lucky not to be hanged, having left a man to bleed to death after a vicious and unwarranted attack. He tried many appeals for early release from the hardships of prison life, and suffered there from heart problems. He wrote many letters to influential people in an attempt to get the case re-opened, and strenuously denied killing Wall, asserting strongly that Wall had died from the fall from the footplate, but there was not enough weight or compulsion to persuade the authorities to take up the case again.

45
Little boy lost,
little boy murdered

*T*he discovery of the body of a 5-year-old child under the seat of a train on the Chalk Farm to Broad Street line of the old North London Railway touched the hearts of many who read of the tragedy in the national press in January 1914. The body was that of Willie Starchfield, whose father John Starchfield lived alone in a common lodging house in Long Acre, his estranged wife Agnes living in lodgings in Hampstead Road, Camden.

Mrs Starchfield was an out-of-work tailoress and on the day in question she had gone out to find work, leaving her delicate little son with her landlady, Mrs Emily Longstaff. Willie was a bright little lad, angelic in appearance with his long curly hair like that of a girl. He got on well with Mrs Longstaff and she sent him on an errand to a stationer's shop just down Hampstead Road. However, he had not returned when his mother came home at 3 pm.

John Starchfield's life had had its dramatic moments. He sold newspapers at his pitch on the corner of Oxford Street and Tottenham Court Road for some 16 years, but his moment of glory came on 27 September 1912 when a mad Armenian tailor, Stephen Titus, went mad with a revolver in the bar of the Horseshoe Hotel in Tottenham Court Road, killing the manageress. As Titus charged into the street, Starchfield tackled him and brought him down. Titus regained his feet and shot John Starchfield in the stomach, nearly killing him. Starchfield suffered agonies with the wound for several years, but for his bravery he was awarded a pound a week from the Carnegie Hero Fund.

As a husband, however, he was a dead loss. He had no sense of responsibility and treated his wife badly until she left him to make her own way in life. He had been in prison twice for failing to pay his wife maintenance, and now his pound a week award was paid direct to Agnes. They had lost two children and Willie was the apple of Agnes's eye, a dear little boy. John Starchfield had a heavy dark moustache, Italian looks and mesmeric eyes.

It did not take the police long to identify that the body was that of Willie. The medical evidence suggested that death had occurred between 2 and 3 pm, but they could not be sure as to whether the boy had been strangled on the train or had been killed and his pathetic little body dumped on any train in the vicinity. The police were soon questioning John Starchfield, but he did not seem unduly upset when told about his only son's death. He said that he had not been in the Camden area that afternoon, and could prove it, as he had been in bed until 3.30 pm feeling unwell with his old wound. A fellow lodger, William Tilley, had been in the same room until 3 pm.

Public interest was naturally considerable in cases of children's ill-treatment and murder, and this incident was no exception. The inquest opened on 15 January, and it was clear that the police had been busy with their investigations. A length of cord had been found on the side of the railway line near Broad Street railway station, and Dr Bernard Spilsbury, the eminent pathologist, thought that it might just be the cord that had been used to strangle Willie. George Jackson, a signalman operating St Pancras Junction box halfway between Camden Town and Maiden Lane stations, said that he saw a man in a train leaning over a form of someone who had fair, curly hair – he thought it was a girl. The time would have been 2.07 pm.

Another important witness was Mrs Clara Wood, who saw a man resembling Starchfield with a little boy who was eating a cake on the corner of Angler's Lane about 1.15 pm. When she had seen the newspaper account of Dr Spilsbury's inquest and the analysis of the contents of the boy's stomach, which stated that it contained cake, she had reported the incident to the police; she had bought a coconut cake just like the one she had seen the little boy eating, and she showed it to Dr Spilsbury who said it was very like the remains of the cake in Willie's stomach. This very damning evidence was further compounded when she was asked by the Coroner if she had seen the man since. Mrs Wood, in a most dramatic gesture, flung out her arm and pointed at John Starchfield; her eyes blazing, she declared, 'Yes, there'.

Another witness then identified Starchfield in court. Richard White, a commercial traveller, declared that at around 2 pm on 8 January he had seen an Italian-looking man with a thin, fragile little boy at the booking office at Camden Town station. He, too, pointed at Starchfield and said, 'That's the man I saw'.

Starchfield vigorously denied the accusations, but did not convince the Coroner's jury, and was charged with murder. The trial began at the Old Bailey on 31 March, but at the end of the case brought by the prosecution the Judge directed the jury to acquit Starchfield on the grounds that the case revolved entirely on evidence of identity, which was not acceptable. Starchfield was a hero once more, and was cheered by the crowd as he left the Old Bailey. He died two years later from the effects of the bullet wound in his stomach.

The murder of Willie Starchfield remains unsolved, but Chief Inspector William Gough, who was involved in the case from beginning to end, was sure that Starchfield had killed his son, that he had abducted him to cause his wife pain and worry. Willie, however, had not co-operated and had not wanted to go with his father. Starchfield had bought him a cake to placate him and had taken him to Camden Town station at around 2 pm. Once aboard the train, Gough surmised, Willie had started to cry and bawl, his father had lost his temper and had struck him. Willie had bawled even louder and in order to shut him up his father had strangled him with the piece of cord he used to tie up newspapers.

Starchfield vehemently denied all allegations that he had harmed his own son, and one of his theories was that Stephen Titus, the mad Armenian, had killed his son as an act of revenge. The police did not believe this story but, strangely, Starchfield's solicitor found three witnesses who swore that they saw near Hampstead Road a little boy who resembled Willie being taken by the hand by a woman at about 1 pm. The boy and the woman had also been seen on a bus that took them to Chalk Farm station.

It was never proved where the murder had taken place, whether on the train or at some other place, then the body dumped on the floor of the carriage. If Starchfield had done the foul deed, one wonders what might have come into a father's mind to make him murder his only son. We shall never know.

46
The St Albans tragedy

I am most grateful to the *Herts Advertiser* for their co-operation in supplying details of this grisly murder. The Great Northern Railway station in London Road, St Albans, was closed to passengers on 1 October 1951, but it remained open to goods traffic and parcels until final closure came on 5 October 1964. The old building was the setting for the murder of Mr Joseph Ellingham, who back in August 1918 was the Station Master.

The Great War was drawing towards its bloody close and the world held its breath as negotiations to bring the carnage to an end continued. The role of a Station Master in those days was somewhat different to the present-day situation. Mr Ellingham was the head of a team of porters, clerks and other members of staff who operated this busy station, and was revered and respected by his colleagues and friends.He was also a keen gardener, devoting much of his free time to the garden that adjoined the building. He had 'green fingers' and was successful in growing considerable crops of fruit, vegetables and flowers; indeed, his skill as a grower of carnations and lilies was known far and wide, and his skills had been commented upon in the gardening press. He was never happier than when in his beloved garden.

Mrs Ellingham, however, was a very unhappy person and found it difficult to get on with anybody; she worried about everything and everybody, and found fault with most things in life. She quarrelled with her husband and her family, and perhaps that was one reason why her husband preferred to work as much as possible in the garden!

Mr Ellingham also studied railways in general. He was most particular that St Albans station was meticulously clean and tidy, and that his staff were clean, polite and efficient. He had been offered promotion to another station, but when his public found out they presented a petition to the GNR imploring them to let him stay at St Albans. Mr Ellingham's duties also included those of local Traffic Superintendent, and his efficiency in these duties was also duly appreciated.

It was therefore a great shock to all when the news of Mr Ellingham's death became known. His horribly battered body was found in his upstairs sitting room, his body lying partly under the table and blood-soaked cushions around his head. The station staff were concerned when he had not appeared to superintend the departure of the 2.45 pm train – he was usually most particular about attending train arrivals and departures. The concern grew as the day went on and there was still no sign of him. Evening came, but his daughter Mabel would be home from her work soon, then any worries would be cleared up. However, at 7 pm the staff were so worried that a ladder was found and one of the porters climbed up to see if anything could be seen in the private quarters; strangely, nothing untoward was observed.

At about 8.30 pm Miss Mabel Ellingham arrived home from her job at the local bakery, and authorised a forced entry into the house. Mr Archer, the chief clerk, Mr Allsop, of the goods department, and one of the porters went in to look around, and came across the shocking sight of Mr Ellingham lying dead; the chief injury seemed to be a puncture wound below his left ear. It would appear that he had been resting on a sofa – he had been unwell recently and had to rest – and it looked as though he had been attacked while he was asleep. Moreover, Mrs Ellingham was found in a collapsed state hanging over a gas ring from which gas was still emanating. One of the clerks managed to get her into a chair; she was alive but only semi-conscious and making 'a moaning noise'. She had been deliberately inhaling gas, probably in a determination to commit suicide.

Later the daughter, Mabel, said that she lived with her parents and had been temporarily employed at a local bakery in Victoria Street, St Albans. She had last seen her father just before she left home for work; he was having his breakfast. She did not see her mother. On arriving home at around 8.30 pm she could not get into the house and asked Mr Archer, the chief clerk, if he would help her to get in; it was then that she had seen her father's body.

On the kitchen table was a note in her mother's hand, but she did not read it. The note read as follows: 'I am sorry for you all. It is a good thing that you have a home of your own to go to and I hope you will be happy now that I am out of your way. With your father's money and mine you may be able to do without going out to earn your living – not like poor me who had to work to help to keep this station and in my old days I had no love or comfort. So goodbye to you all. I am taking him with me. Don't forget he has some money of Uncle Ted's. You had better give it to your Uncle Dan to take care of for him.'

The inquest proceedings at St Albans Town Hall were of a quiet nature. A group of relatives of the deceased sat at the back of the hall, and the inquest was opened at 10.30 am by Dr Lovall Drage, the Coroner. The jury consisted of eight persons, Mr Gerald J. C. Dracon, of the GNR Solicitors Department at King's Cross, represented the railway company, but the general public was little represented. The first witness was John Ellingham, son of the deceased. He said that his father was 61 years of age and was Station Master at the Great Northern railway station at St Albans. He last saw his father at noon on Friday 16 August, when Mr Ellingham senior passed the office window at which his son worked in Victoria Street. John called at his father's station home at about 5.40 pm with the local paper as usual, but found the side door, which he always used, locked and bolted.

Mabel Ellingham added that her father had always been a steady, reliable, hard-working man. She had lived with her parents all her life; there had been differences, but her mother had always caused the trouble. Her mother had suffered from delusions and had made her father's life very difficult; he had shown great tolerance, but possibly his obsession with his garden did not exactly improve matters. Miss Ellingham identified the letter written by her mother, and the Coroner said, 'These letters are all the same – even I have one. She must have written innumerable letters to everyone she could think of. Mrs Ellingham's mental condition will have to be examined by her Doctor.'

The Coroner mentioned a very strong smell of spirits arising from the deceased body; a glass of beer was on the table together with a syphon of soda water three parts full. A glass chimney and globe was also on the table, and next to it was an envelope on which was written in pencil: 'My daughter Mabel's cruel treatment'. The deceased right eye was black and his nose was bent as if broken. In the kitchen were four more letters addressed in pencil to Connie, Rose, John and Mabel, while on the kitchen table was an uneaten meal, cutlery, and a dish containing tapioca. In the coal scuttle near the fire was a heavy hammer stamped 'GNR' with bloodstains on the head and shaft, and there were seven wounds on the deceased's head that had obviously been caused by the hammer.

The next day the Coroner visited the house again accompanied by Superintendent Peck, and in the deceased's bedroom they found a bloodstained skirt and a blouse with blood on it. The water in the hand basin was discoloured as if someone had tried to wash off bloodstains, and more blood had splashed all round the floor and curtains.

The doctor's report said that he had examined the body in the mortuary and found four abrasions on the nose and two over the right eye; one on the forehead had penetrated to the bone, and there were also seven puncture wounds in the skull and two at the back of the head. These wounds had been caused by a blunt instrument. A blackening blood clot on the face indicated that some acid had been poured over it, and death had been caused by shock.

Addressing the jury the Coroner said there was not much doubt that the unfortunate man's death had been caused by repeated blows with the heavy hammer wielded by Mrs Ellingham. Indeed, the savage frenzy she must have been in at the time must have been terrifying. She was obviously deranged; jealousy, which had long been a problem with her, had developed into a fixed delusion, and this had turned into homicidal mania. There was not enough evidence to show that she was sane at the time of the murder; the jury's verdict was 'Wilful Murder', and Mrs Ellingham was committed to a mental hospital for the rest of her life.

47
Two peas in a pod

David had shown an interest in money matters from a very early age, and his parents had encouraged him to save from his weekly pocket money. They had given him a rather novel money box – it was shaped like a small book with brass sides and had a small key that was kept at the local bank. They would take the money box into town and the Bank Manager would open it up and count the proceeds and enter it in David's Bank book; David would then pocket the box and the family would resume their shopping and eventually go back to the station and board their train home.

David was above average academically, went to the local Grammar School, did well in his final exams and was fortunate enough to get a job as a Junior Clerk in a bank. He eventually worked his way up into the higher echelons and became Chief Clerk at a branch in the City of London.

His interest in railways also developed over the years – he travelled extensively to all parts of the United Kingdom by rail and collected items of railwayana of which he was justly proud. His great pleasure was the rail journeys that he made to and from London on company business; he would see all manner of locomotives and stock, and the large stations fascinated him. The railway system held so much interest – he often wondered whether he should have joined one of the railway companies instead of the often austere atmosphere of banking.

It was in the spring of 1938 that David was offered the post of Assistant Manager of a small branch of the bank in the Highlands of Scotland. David loved Scotland and the scenic beauty of the Highlands and gladly accepted the position. Within the month he was journeying through the glens behind a wheezy old tank engine to the little town. David soon settled down in his new surroundings; he found good digs and a kind elderly lady who treated him as her own.

He also found himself the target of the local girls, and was soon an established member of the local community. They played tennis, darts and golf, went walking in the nearby glens and generally did what most young people of their age did. He found himself rather enamoured by a young girl called Elizabeth a farmer's daughter who lived in a remote old farmhouse nearby.

David had found other interests by then and he played the clarinet in a local jazz band, playing in and around the nearby villages, and Elizabeth would come and smile at him from her seat in the front row. She was very pretty, with a nice smile and long blonde hair, and it was not long before he was seeing a lot of her.

On being invited up to the farm he was astonished when Elizabeth introduced her twin sister Fiona. David stood and gaped – he had never seen two girls so alike – like two peas in a pod. The strange thing was that David found that when he visited the farm or took Elizabeth home after a date, if he turned his back he wondered if he was kissing Elizabeth or Fiona good night, especially if, as was likely, they were wearing identical clothes.

David would have married Elizabeth if the Second World War had not intervened. He enlisted in the RAF and went abroad; letters became difficult and the two young people drifted apart. Eventually David was demobbed and returned to banking. He was given a branch in the outskirts of London, but he had never forgotten Elizabeth and at his first opportunity he took the train up to the Highlands.

The railways had changed dramatically. Having been run down by the wartime emergency, the well-cared-for stations were now drab and dirty, the coaches were in need of refurbishment and the locomotives were unkempt and ill-maintained. Nevertheless, he enjoyed the journey and wondered what sort of welcome he would receive from his former girlfriend. He was in for a surprise, for Elizabeth had married a much older man, a mill-owner with considerable wealth, but when they met their eyes told of a love affair that was very much still alive.

Elizabeth told David that her mother had died during the war and that her father was now very old and frail. Fiona was still living at and working the farm, and was still single. David found a love for her that only equalled his similar love for her sister. He therefore started courting Fiona, travelling the long-distance rail journey from London as often as he could, she visiting him in London when she was free.

A little while later they married. Happiness was, however, to turn to sorrow towards Christmas of that same year when Elizabeth's husband Bernard died, followed by the girls' father six weeks later. Fiona was still running the farm and they decided to put it up for sale. David had been trying to get a transfer to a branch of the bank in Scotland, as meetings were getting very difficult. Unfortunately the farm would not sell and David missed his wife – the long train journey was tiring and arduous.

Then one weekend Fiona came down to see him, and they spent a pleasant time just on their own. She talked about things before the war and David realised that she had had a long conversation with Elizabeth. When she left to catch the train home, David found that the love between them was as strong as ever. The mill was being run by a manager, but Elizabeth had tired of the problems of running the business, and eventually contracts were drawn up for its sale, and Elizabeth would soon become a very rich woman.

The new owners sent samples of cloth down to London for delivery to their factory in the Home Counties. The cloth would be packed in large wooden crates, and for speedy delivery these were sent by express passenger trains and were collected at King's Cross; the crates were usually sent twice or three times a week. Fiona had planned another weekend visit to see David and thought it would be good for Elizabeth to accompany her, to which her sister readily agreed. We can only guess that the carriage of three crates in the guard's van on the same train as the two sisters had been planned by Elizabeth, for on arrival at King's Cross only Elizabeth and two crates left the train. The third crate has been re-labelled en route and now bore the address of the farm in the Highlands.

Fiona was never seen again. Or was she? What went on in the guard's van on that March day we will never know. Fiona – or was it Elizabeth? – returned to the farm the following Monday in time to receive the crate, which arrived on the Wednesday of that week. The farm was sold at last to a property developer who demolished it and built holiday cottages on the site. Was this the unfortunate twin's last resting place? Had Fiona killed Elizabeth to get David finally for herself? Or had the jealous Elizabeth killed her sister, seeing Fiona as a threat to her marriage? We shall never know.

David and his wife were now very wealthy indeed, as the proceeds from the sale of the farm and the mill kept them in comfort. So does crime pay? And did David really know the true identity of his wife? Again, we shall never know.

48
Deabled infatuation

The Glasgow Herald of Wednesday 30 August 1944 records the sentence of 10 years penal servitude on a railway carter found guilty of the murder of a 30-year-old woman who was employed by the LNER as a checker in the same goods station where he worked. She had worked there for the last four years, checking goods in and out, and the carter had made friends with her; he had showed her how to lift heavy articles in a safe way and had instructed her in other safety methods that prevented injury. Apparently the friendship had grown between them and soon he found that he had the problem of concealing the relationship from his wife. Whether in fact the affair was serious or just an infatuation is debatable, but the fact seems to be that a close relationship had developed.

Eventually the carter's wife found out and he had a lot of explaining to do at home. She begged her errant husband to break off the relationship and do the decent thing – he had a daughter of 20 and seemed to love his wife. Her husband promised that he would end the affair – but he did not say how. He had a good record in his job, he was thought of as reliable and of good character, but it would seem that the other woman had a mesmeric effect on his emotions, and the clandestine affair carried on amid the bustle of arrivals and departures of goods traffic.

The carter, it appears, did try to break off the relationship at one time; to placate his wife's feelings, he put in for a transfer to another part of the railway, but just at that time there were no vacancies, so he had to stay where he was. The woman's influence seemed to attract him whenever he saw her and he felt helplessly in love with her. However, on the afternoon of 15 June Railway Police Constable Donald McVean saw the couple standing at a gate talking loudly. McVean assumed from the heated discussion that things were far from friendly; he also saw the couple talking on one of the goods platforms. As he completed his round of inspection he saw what appeared to be a shadow in one of the LNER goods vans. He went into the van and shone his torch into the dark recesses, and there he saw a man and woman lying in the corner. For a moment he thought they were 'spooning', and went and told the supervisor that he was not happy with the situation. The supervisor accompanied him back to the van, went in first and asked the carter what was going on. The latter replied that the woman was dead. A closer look revealed her swollen face and froth dribbling from her mouth. The man got up and said, 'She's having her last sleep.' He walked to the door and said, 'I think you ought to call the police.'

He appeared to be completely rational and calm; indeed, he had the reputation fro being a very popular man with great strength. When Railway Police Sergeant Harmison arrived the carter said to him, 'It's no use trying to revive her. I made sure she was finished.'

At his trial, the Defence tried to play down the charge of murder; they offered the possibility of a sudden personality change emanating from extreme infatuation that made the accused act so savagely. He had leapt on to the woman, grabbing her by the throat and squeezing the life out of her. This show of extreme violence was completely contrary to his otherwise equable personality, and he could not account for his alien actions. Nevertheless the charge was murder, and many questions had to be answered.

The Defence's case that the accused was insane at the time was debatable, but they offered the plea of diminished responsibility. Having admitted the charge that he killed the woman, he left his Defence counsel to try to mitigate the circumstances. He had hitherto stuck to his plea of not guilty of murder, but after consideration his legal advisers brought in the plea of 'culpable homicide', which was common in Scottish law, the equivalent of 'second degree murder'. This laid emphasis on the *blame* attached to the act of killing, but certainly did not exonerate the accused from the dreadful deed. It did, however, enable him to escape the early morning walk to meet the hangman.

After all the evidence had been heard, Defence Counsel urged once more the fact of his diminished sense of mental responsibility at the time when he suddenly turned from feelings of extreme passion to the unstoppable desire to choke the life out of his lover. The court was told of the complete absence of premeditation, but the desire to break off this emotional association. The Judge, in passing sentence, said that the accused was under the influence of a passionate infatuation, which played havoc in the lives of many men. It appeared that accused had been the subject of ridicule by the woman, and he was extremely sensitive to this, but what he did was out of all proportion to his feelings. Not long before this terrible act of extreme violence took place, the couple had been laughing and the relationship had seemed normal; then a sudden, overpowering and quite unpremeditated impulse had overtaken the man, and he had acted completely out of character. The Judge pronounced against the accused the sentence of 10 years' penal servitude.

It would appear that he had been lucky to escape the death sentence. The plea of insanity, later changed to that of diminished responsibility, had placed doubt in the jury's minds, but it is interesting that the Judge passed down the sentence of 10 years' penal servitude, a term of imprisonment that would not have been used for a man either insane or of diminished responsibility. Perhaps it is always easy to be wise after the event!

49
Culpable homicide on the Aberdeen express

A few days before Christmas 1950 the express for Aberdeen left Edinburgh Waverley at 2.15 in the afternoon. In those early post-war days many service personnel used the train services travelling to and from leave or postings; the timetable was improving gradually and the trains were slowly gaining their pre-war prestige in timekeeping and general comfort. So what is so interesting about the 2.15 pm Edinburgh-Aberdeen train on that raw, windy day in 1950? It was just another ordinary winter's day for most people, but for one person it was to be her last day on this earth.

A 28-year-old WRAF Corporal was travelling home to see her parents for Christmas. She was stationed at RAF Leuchars and she had joined the train there, travelling to her parents' house in Aberdeen. She was looking forward to the Christmas holiday, and spending it with her parents, with whom she spent most of her leaves. She was a widow; having married just after the war, barely four months later her soldier husband accidentally drowned in a swimming pool accident. To help pick the pieces after this terrible shock she concentrated on her career in the RAF.

Soon after the train left Arbroath a passenger complained to the guard that the toilet had been occupied for an inordinate time. The guard knocked on the door and a voice answered; the door opened and a man came out. The guard could see through the open door that someone else was in the confined space – it was a woman, and she appeared to be dead. He pulled her out and tried to give her artificial respiration, but to no avail – she was dead.

The train arrived at Aberdeen at 6.30 pm, about 40 minutes behind schedule, and CID officers there took charge. The man on the train was arrested. He had been escorting the dead woman since her husband died, but the relationship was a bit 'on/off' – they got together during their spells of leave, and had much in common, both being fond of most sports activities. He was estranged from his wife and, in spite of his entreaties, she refused to divorce him. He wanted to marry the young widow, but while his wife remained obdurate the situation was most frustrating. He too had been on his way home to spend Christmas with his family in Aberdeen.

He was charged with the murder and was remanded in custody to await his trial. By the time he appeared in court early in the New Year the murder charge had been dropped, and one of 'culpable homicide' substituted. A month later he was back in court on a charge of assaulting the dead woman by seizing her and compressing her throat and killing her on a train travelling between Edinburgh and Aberdeen. It was stated to the court that medical evidence showed that this was not a case that could be indicted for murder, as there was no evidence of any intent to kill. Counsel stated 'that the violence used did not display such recklessness as would show complete disregard for the consequences'. The Lord Advocate was of the opinion that the marks on the woman's throat indicated that only a minor degree of violence had been apparent, and that the affair had been more of minor assault. Counsel then stated that the accused and the deceased had planned to spend their Christmas leave together in Aberdeenshire. This was strange, as the accused had said that he was to spend the Christmas holiday with his estranged wife.

The train was pretty full and the two lovers had to stand for a while, then they started quarrelling and other travellers observed a row taking place. Raised voices travel far in a crowded train, and even with the attendant noise and movement of people pushing past each other to regain their seats, evidence has it that the sounds of two screams were heard in the coach next to the toilet. When the guard knocked on the toilet door to enquire what was happening, the man staggered out in a very distressed state and the woman's body was discovered.

Medical evidence stated that she had been suffering from a cardiac inhibition that might have rendered her more vulnerable to shock than a normal person. It was stated at the trial that the row was about the man's broken promise not to drink rum; things got heated and tempers flared. The woman lost her temper when he told her to shut up, and she smacked his face. He then put his hand on her throat and throttled her – the shock would have probably been enough to kill her.

Two senior RAF officers gave the accused good references, and spoke of his good service record and hitherto good character. Counsel then offered the information that his wife was willing to take him back to resume a normal married life when the trial ended. In the event the accused's plea of 'culpable homicide' was accepted instead of the 'capital murder' charge; without doubt he was guilty of the woman's death. The Judge sentenced him to 9 months imprisonment, a very light sentence given the enormity of the crime.

Was this case a crime of passion? Or was it a mere accident? Certainly the killer acted on an impulse, possibly driven on by fury at the woman's scorn and reaction. It is easy to believe his plea that he did not want to kill her, and that he lost his temper in the heat of the moment. Not a killer, more of the victim of circumstance.